GILGAMESH PLAYS

GILGAMESH PLAYS

The Tower of Gilgamesh
&
The Acts of Gilgamesh

JONATHAN BAYLISS

DRAWBRIDGE PRESS

Library of Congress Control Number: 2018937489

ISBN: 978-0-9831504-3-5 (paper)

ISBN: 978-0-9831504-4-2 (cloth)

ISBN: 978-0-9974641-0-8 (epub)

ISBN: 978-0-9974641-2-2 (Kindle)

CONTENTS

These two plays derive from the Sumerian Gilgamesh epic. Each may be produced independently of the other, except that the director of the second one *(The Acts of Gilgamesh)* should be aware of the introductory pages of the first *(The Tower of Gilgamesh)*, which provide notes for the original quasi-legendary mise-en-scène and suggested casting.

THE ACTS OF GILGAMESH

"I have given Enlil a ladder down to earth, and the whole Sea-Land a beacon for caravans and boats. It flashes blue sunbeams into the deep of the sky, and its shadow walks across the city to cool the heads of children."
—   Gilgamesh to Rector, *Tower of Gilgamesh*

"I don't claim fame for madcap feats . . . or for the love of Lil-Amin . . . but there will be space enough in time between my extinction and the world's . . . for arts not handed down from heaven! . . . —Don't let thoughts be lost to time. . . . You must be my voice until Enheduanna writes her poem. . . ."
—   Gilgamesh to Shepherd, *Acts of Gilgamesh*

Gilgamesh is the hero of the world's oldest literary document, a Sumerian epic on clay tablets looking back a thousand years or more from about 2700 BCE. Sumer occupied what is now southern Iraq, where civilization is said to have begun.

THE TOWER OF GILGAMESH

OR

THE ISO-RECTO-TETRAHEDRON

A Comedy for Actors or Dancers

PERSONS AND MASKS

Lil-Amin, queen of Uruk, priestess of Inanna

College of Widows, hierodules of the Temple

The Rector of the Temple, priest of Inanna, formerly governor of Uruk

Optimates, a council of ephors representing the people

Gilgamesh [Giszax], king-errant of Erech [Uruk]

Norkid, captain of his Kassite guard

Troopers, Kassite bowmen of the guard

Eber, Gilgamesh's vizier and patriarch of nomads

Traders, sons of Eber, nomadic merchants

Engidu [Enkidu], a wild man from the steppes

GLOSSARY

	Men's Language	Women's Language
Erech = Uruk (a city in Sumer)	**Err**-ek	Ur-**uk**
Ishtar = Inanna (city goddess)	**Ish**-tar	In-an-**na**
Enlil (the high god)	**En**-lil	En-**lil**
Lil-Amin	**Lil**-a-min	Lil-**ah**-min
Engidu = Enkidu	**En**-gi-du	En-ki-**du**
Gilgamesh = Giszax	**Gil**-ga-mesh	Gee-**zax**

PRODUCTION NOTES

General Desiderata

In principle this is a play for actors who may also be dancers, but in practice it may as well be done by actors few or none of whom are dancers. It would be a fine thing if musicians playing derabucca drums or Indian cymbals, and a flute or recorder, could be sitting on the stage throughout the performance; but music may be otherwise provided, electronically if necessary, as long as the apparatus is not concealed. In a full-scale production, each of the four choruses (Widows, Troopers, Traders, and Optimates) would consist of three or more persons; but in any cast they must equal each other in the number of at least two each.

Suggestions for Casting or Masking

GILGAMESH: cleanshaven.

ENGIDU: black, red, or dark; shaggy and lithe, but muscular or otherwise athletically impressive.

EBER: bearded, longhaired; elderly but vigorous.

RECTOR: perhaps hairless; remarkably strong (even if short); maybe tattooed.

LIL-AMIN: dark; preferably tall and slender.

NORKID: fairhaired; stocky or burly; wears steel-rim eyeglasses.

WIDOWS: lightly wimpled or veiled.

Notation

Dialogues shown in italics are spoken or chanted in unison. In choral parts not individually specified, dashes at the beginning of clauses indicate an arbitrary alternation of speakers.

Properties

Gilgamesh's *axe:* standard double-bitted steel head on a straight wooden haft.

Engidu's *bannerstone:* a primitive symmetrically winged stone mounted on a short throwing handle.

Engidu's *bow and arrow:* the two-part tool used to make fire—a drilling device. (The Troopers use classic English *longbows*.)

The *Iso-recto-tetrahedron:* a solid formed by the corner of a cube, its perpendicular edges of equal length, its oblique face forming an equilateral triangle; threaded with a hole and small enough to wear around the neck on a thong or chain.

Design Criteria

Ad lib: any style from extreme simplicity of set and costume (freely anachronistic, with never more than hints of historical verisimilitude) to sparely ornamented expression of cultural contrast—as long as it is consonant with the idea that this is a play about dancers, not opera singers. (The basic dress may be leotards of solid colors that each characterize one of the four choruses.) Individual masks may be simply or elaborately distinctive.

PROLOGUE

Herodotus of Halicarnassus hereby acknowledges that he was fatally unable to keep the promise in his book about Persia to write a more ancient History of Mesopotamia and Canaan.

I had wished to take entire leave of my own millennium and trace to their origins or antitheses the vestigial myths and rituals I mentioned in the work on Europe, Africa, and Asia that has come down to you. With waxing excitement I was advancing my researches, but had grown weary of the narrative form, which no longer seemed appropriate to my matter, when death overtook me.

The play you are about to see, my first and only attempt at drama, was the last thing I ever wrote, though only the introduction to my project. I was hoping to have it produced at the Greater Dionysia of the year you would designate as the 431st before your era, but I was debarred from competition both because of my disallowed Athenian citizenship (on the basis of a dead-letter law) and because, lacking poetic credentials, I was presumed to know nothing about the theater worthy of anybody's investment. In any case, my manuscript was disqualified when the archon refused to recognize it as comedy or satyr play, let alone tragedy.

Anyway, that year I would have found myself in rivalry with *Oedipus Tyrannus.* I was not terribly distressed that the battered scroll of my play, having been mistaken for mere notes to a History that would never be written, was burned at my funeral in Thuria as a symbolic sacrifice by my beloved wife.

For centuries I was called the father of lies; but your scholars have revived interest in our common cultural origins and therewith justified many of my conjectures about barbarian peoples and places denied or ignored by the proud Athenians, whose western seapower blinded them to the formative influence of Sumer, of which Akkad, Assyria, and the Babylon I visited were but imperial degenerations.

At the time of legendary Gilgamesh, a couple of thousand years before Semiramis and her even greater successor Nitocris (who made a labyrinth of the upper Euphrates to protect her Babylon from riverain invaders), the Sumerian city of Uruk—known in your Bible as Erech, especially sacred to Enlil (the original Bel or Baal), indigenous father of the gods, and to his daughter Inanna (later Ishtar)—was upstream hegemon of the eastern Sea-Lands. It was a time when the Tigris and Euphrates still debouched separately into the reedy silt-marshes of the Gulf that has since been named the Persian—almost as far from the splendid concerns of Pericles in miles as in years.

As you know from Boethius and others, those two rivers arose from the Ararat rocks, near alpine Lake Van, which remains more central to the world than Greece itself. I believe that in Sumer, at the bottom of that double-rivered plain, west of Eden, mankind first invented agriculture, writing, and other technology. The myths of Gilgamesh, or Giszax, began in pre-Semitic Sumerian ritual.

At some point an historical tyrant may have taken upon himself that famous name, perhaps as that of a traditional conqueror from the Zagros Mountains; but it's more likely that the primeval stories accrued to a born king Gilgamesh of the world's first city. In Babylon I heard an epic poem, a latterday redaction; but it seems to have simplified the tensions and conflicts that Gilgamesh must have experienced at the fountainhead of culture, where not merely two streams divided, but three or even four.

TABLET
ONE

[Between dawn and sunrise. The square in front of Gilgamesh's headquarters.]

Enter Widows, sauntering.

WIDOW 1   A Widow praying to get pregnant!
Don't you realize what it means to get
expelled? Where's your self-respect
when you've lost the emoluments and
perquisites of College? You'll be out of
the cold into the frozen. I tell you this
dearth of work is just a time of passing
troubles!

WIDOW 2   Passing troubles! What's passing are the
ways handed down from heaven by the
Lord God Enlil! I've heard the next
thing Giszax wants to change is time
itself!

WIDOW 1   How could he change the seasons of
women? We shall outlive him. It's the
worst of times for us to act capricious!

WIDOW 2   My vocation isn't strong enough to endure depression. What's the joy in an easy life if there aren't as many worshippers as couches? Don't preach to me about my career! The trouble is I like too much what we all profess. I can't be content with mere gestures of what we're here for! Under Giszax's yoke the clients of Inanna are as wilted as our sun-stroked bulls and rams. Bonded marriage is better than watered-down religious life—if I can land some crippled smith or leach who won't be drafted, or a boy with the enthusiasm not yet sweated out of him by godless labor! I'll earn my wrinkles spinning flax for an only child and at least half a man.

WIDOW 1   A helot's life is hell. You'll make a sorry housewife. Domestic wool is frayed before it's woven. And you're mistaken if you think Inanna will bless desertion. But say you do squeeze out one live baby: you can't expect a sister or a brother for her—when all the life around grows barren from our conquering savior's love of sacrilege!

WIDOW 2   While you sit by and watch Lil-Amin weave herself a dole of bitterest humiliation. I'm tired of weeping for our own queen confined to tapestries—while a self-appointed shah usurps the prerogatives of gods! For seven years her moons have come and gone—and still she's our priest in name alone. Giszax might as well have walled her up with bricks!

WIDOW 1   But the Rector's spindle isn't yet unwound! Soon he'll seize back the Rod and Ring. In fact, I just heard—

WIDOW 2   I wouldn't mind the family way at all. I'd like to get to really know a man— maybe even one of Giszax's palefaced falangists . . .

WIDOW 1   But listen to this—

WIDOW 2   You always listen to those hoaxes on ourselves. What kind of oracle can be brought to pass by gossip? You should have given up hope when Giszax took the warhead off his axe and proclaimed himself our peacemaker. It appears that peace consists of a law and order that tampers with the language, doctors our numbers, and desecrates our calendar. *Enter troopers, unobserved, listening to the Widows.* Better be at war than have our unison deranged. No sacrifice by the Rector will ever again raise my hope against a planting by the sun. Giszax's hideous obsessions darken the streets and regiment the waters.

WIDOW 1   Inanna will send us a champion! I'm telling you—

WIDOW 2   Oh please excuse me! I thought you were going to say the goddess herself, on second thought, would strike him dead! —Oh, oh! Don't look up. The Kassites are spying again!

TROOPER 1   Our forbidden fruit off guard!

TROOPER 2   If it ain't the bachelor girls bewailing their famine! Such sad song was never heard.

TROOPER 1   Hello, miladies! Are your coffers empty?

WIDOW 1   Did I hear hyenas yapping?

WIDOW 2   It's only the melting snowmen. From time to time they make attempts at speech.

TROOPER 2   They forget we saved their honor from the Elamites. Chivalry is but a trifle in this depraved witchburg!

TROOPER 1   We could cheer you up, bellibones!

WIDOW 1   No matter how long they study Uruk, these hillbillies will never be anything but unconscionable barbarians.

TROOPER 1   Un-con-shun-a-bul? Sounds like illegal woman-talk.

TROOPER 2   Or one of the Captain's words. We must be as uncouth as they say we are.

WIDOW 1   I could excuse simple ignorance, but not willful stupidity. They can't tell cashmere from earthenware. Ridiculous Chanticleers, to strut the ramparts crowing all their smut!

WIDOW 2   They do seem hardly chaste. But maybe where they come from—

WIDOW 1   Uncircumcised boars, bragging about their stinkhorns! But from what I hear on the outside, when it comes to business, these flagging dildoes only peck and bolt.

TROOPER 1   You must have a sweet-tooth somewhere, little jailbait!

WIDOW 1   I don't dote on fungus, and I've never had a yen for albino-livered chalk-skinned turnkeys.

TROOPER 1   It's not by choice we're on penal duty. And you're wrong if you guess I'm white all over. Want to see, Miss Bigot?

WIDOW 1   I know all about these parade-ground sharks: they're shrimps in battle. Super-annuated striplings! They come and go with the stamina of rotten bananas. Doughboys reared on halfbaked under-leavened bread. It's a poor brave that proves his manhood by the scalps he's left alive. The kind that shoots on sight but leaves his victim tossing!

WIDOW 2   Perhaps they need a governess. My grandmother said that pioneers who only plow never learn to sow and reap.

TROOPER 2   I'd be happy to have the harvest of your tutoring.

WIDOW 2   It's only right that what is torn should not be left unmended.

TROOPER 1   If Gilgamesh would let me, I'd show you how bowmen till shrewish whores sodden with their cultivation!

WIDOW 1   The bombastic hounds of Giszax are yapping on the leash! Let's go, before the feathered shuttlecocks work themselves into a lather and dribble out their curdless scum.

Enter Norkid.

TROOPER 1   There's always some battledore to sour a man's pearls.

TROOPER 2   You there, don't scowl! Ishtar bids you love her gifts.

WIDOW 2   I never said I hated them.

WIDOW 1   The bluster of slavedrivers doesn't faze me—but Our Lady preserve us from lewd insolence!

Widows leave.

TROOPER 2   I like the way she walks. A man should be allowed to measure his place with a woman he can get to know. Kids and all.

NORKID   At it again, yardbirds? You can't win a war of words with female churchwardens. The ways of our fathers are forever accursed to Messpot mothers. —*Fall* IN!

[Coming forward.]

TROOPERS

[Forming up in front of Norkid after a little shuffle.]

Let them sing about their law,
But clip the doxies' tooth and claw.
Stitch their backbone to the mat
And make them purr like a pussycat!

NORKID   You cherry-pickers have nothing to gripe about. In my day a dogface would give all his pay for your fatigue duty, cracking the crotch of maidens. —*At-ten*-TION! —You royal guards have nothing to do at night but pluck the rosebuds—while your king takes the watch alone. Gilgamesh stays awake and you get all the sleep!

TROOPER 2   Poor Gilgamesh. He stays awake to think, and never takes the spoils. His nostrils flare no longer.

TROOPER 1   I didn't enlist to police a gang of brick-layers. An engineering king has turned me into a clerk-of-the-works!

NORKID   I'll clerk your works! —*Dress it up* now! —There was a time when you were glad enough for all that tender meat. It made up for lack of plunder. But now you're billeted like gentry, you bitch all day because you're not allowed the common mess. —A-*bout*-FACE!

TROOPER I   The common mess is too rich for its brokendown hod-carriers, while all the military gets is uncooked veal—if the Rector doesn't consecrate it first!

NORKID
[Continuing the
drill with various
commands.]

You used to say variety's the spice of life.

TROOPER I   Fucking little variety in a bushel of green apples! At least on payday I ought to get a bite that's ripe.

TROOPER 2   On these rations a man gets old with nothing but firstborn kids he can't even claim are his. I'd give a year's crop of pullets for one off-limits hen.

TROOPER I   First they squeal, then they bleat. Long black eyelashes full of reproach because we didn't deliver the great swoon they've whispered about since their teats began to swell.

NORKID   *Company* HALT! —Graduation's just commencement.

TROOPER 2   Not for us. We get the girls, but we're not allowed to fraternize with women! We're always starting over. We get the sting so some farmhand can collect the honey!

NORKID   Even on archers in this vale of tears some rain must fall. —*Half-left*-FACE! —You could try a hunger strike.

TROOPER 1   A lion in the cage can't turn up his nose at the daily feed of jackal-food.

TROOPER 2   Who can resist the flowers of spring? It's the foretaste that keeps you ravenous.

NORKID
[Marching them back and forth.]   Even to me, aged and infirm, it's superhuman, how Gilgamesh fights shy of the world's most undeflowered queen— absolutely at his mercy!

TROOPER 1   Now there's a lure to cheerful death! Long legs and inborn talent! How can he keep his distance from the parthenon? I sometimes wonder if he's lost his orchids.

NORKID   Why a king might want to keep his cast is beyond the understanding of caco-ethical billygoats.

TROOPER 1   There he goes again! But I guess I can guess what it means.

TROOPER 2   If Lil-Amin is not his caste, who for god's sake is?

NORKID   *Pre-sent* ARMS!

TROOPER 1   Long arms or short arms?

NORKID   Any more of your lip and I'll present my hammy fist to you! —*Pa-rade* REST! Your style was sharper when ass was scarce.

TROOPERS
[Shuffling their
feet.]

While we work this female city
We'll never know a woman's pity.
So we take the duty with the burden
And settle for the schoolgirl guerdon.

NORKID
[Motioning them
through the
routine of target
practice.]

Things began to get out of kilter when Gilgamesh unstepped his iron eagle with its twin thin lips. Without that axe, before long we'll be fighting with our backs to the winding stairs. —You need more work on form. That's what counts in getting up your speed. To put down a mob, six seconds a shot is much too slow. They must be more quickly reminded of our feathered wood.

TROOPER 1

Inside walls, strings don't make good music! You should be leading us in the sword dance.

NORKID

Swords won't terrify the middle of a crowd. You can talk back after you've learnt how to shoot around corners: meanwhile you've got to stretch your range. Step back another yard.

TROOPER 1

My funnybone's already bumping the wall!

NORKID

I'll put in for your decoration: Knight of the Humerus.

TROOPER 1

Don't make me laugh.

NORKID

Tonight you can cry in your beer. Right now, show me your feathers in the bullseye. You're not past pluperfect yet.

TROOPERS   *Draw that arrow,*
Nock the string.
Loose your shaft
And make it sing!
One, two, three, four—
Back tomorrow to drill some more!

NORKID   Let's *go*, let's GO! You're slower than the pole star.

TROOPER 2   We were young when we followed Gilgamesh down from the north on some vague summons of the night wind to raise a siege of strangers. No one can say the gods didn't warn us. Our shields were too full of holes to float; he led us across the Tigris on wineskins. At first this whole irrigation district welcomed us like a pantheon of liberators. I thought we'd take home their gold, and odalisks to boot!

TROOPER 1   Instead we smother to death in garrison while he spends his time inventing calendars and designing public works. Anyway, what's the tower for? An island for the second coming of their Flood? To watch their enemies from afar? Or to see more stars? Well we can make them tote and stack the bricks, but they won't man it on their own. They think mortals are forbidden to see more than a mile at a time!

Enter Gilgamesh, unobserved, with headless axe-handle in one hand.

TROOPER 2   Gilgamesh can see near and far without a stepladder. I don't see why he should build a tower for gods that hate him.

TROOPER 1   If only he'd keep his mind on the military problem!

NORKID   My military problem is to keep his stormtroopers from going soft, so that by time he's ready to remount his double-bite you'll still be able to hit a temple door. If you're not up to the mark in a little sport like this, you can't expect to save your pampered skins wee-wee-wee all the way home. So there you have your answer: The tower's a refuge for aging archers against a host of pitchforks!

TROOPERS   *Why did our proud demented king*
Accept from them their Rod and Ring?
Why pile a mountain on the plain
To raise on high Lord Enlil's fane?

NORKID   Let's secure this pisspoor muster. Don't let me keep you from your bossing. Go call the roll of masons! Take up your lash! The sooner you top that topless tower off, the better we can hope to return to our life of honorable violence. —*Fall* OUT! On the double now! Don't keep the labor battalion standing around.

TROOPER 1   Hurry up, he says! Hurry up and wait!

TROOPER 2

[Troopers
unhurriedly
prepare to
leave.]

Hurry up the heavy looking-on! Wait for the pace-setter!

GILGAMESH

[Menacing them
mockingly with
his axe-handle.]

Well, well: my elite guard all alert and fresh in the morning dew! A moon-struck nightwalker can surprise them even after sunrise!

TROOPERS

Troopers go out
hastily, dancing
like sentries.

A pace or two, and turn.
Up the stairs and down.
We fiddle on our bows
To pacify this town!

NORKID

Police duty makes simple soldiers iron-ical. But you already knew that. Your wide ear takes in from most to least.

GILGAMESH

Your Kassites have wide mouths.

NORKID

I confess they're not cut out for mar-shalling civilians harmlessly. I'm a little stir-crazy myself. It's been seven years since we've seen a real rock or a moun-tain. The Sea-Land marshes get a little boring.

GILGAMESH

Be of good cheer: you'll soon have for-eign intelligence to amuse you. Eber's spit-and-images are sailing in from the desert with salt and other cargo.

NORKID

Begging your pardon: Hip, hip, hurray for all the excitement.

GILGAMESH   I'd have thought you'd get excited about the failure of your guard to spot their dust before I happened to.

NORKID   You know I don't have enough men for idle masthead watch.

GILGAMESH   Then be glad of these Eberew reinforcements.

NORKID   We don't need a cavalry of merchants. But I hope the peaceloving straight-laced Bactrian-drivers can defend themselves at least.

Enter Eber.

GILGAMESH   They wear shortswords under their veils. —Here's Eber now. If it weren't for this colleague, dear Norkid, where would all my engineering be? He's factored all the timber and stone, and rafted the lintels down river on their own joists!

NORKID   It was your suggestion, sir.

GILGAMESH   Now he's imported our most obscure necessity. Who else would have known that salt could cure sweatiness in men and skinniness in cattle? I had thought we could dispense with trade, once we'd stocked some soapstone and cedar!

EBER   As your humble servants my sons were everywhere received like magi. Your seal made them wizards of finance. From sea to sea, the name of Gilgamesh opened the door of every counting-house and caravansary.

GILGAMESH   My vizier of budgets and accounts is a catholic statesman.

EBER   As your minister I've refrained from censure of the customs here. Have I not dealt justly with all the people?

GILGAMESH   Yes, yes, I always praise your jurisprudence too.

EBER   It used to be that no one ever tried to revive a poor man when he died, because the life he lost wasn't worth retaining. Now he's hired at twice his worth, gets his bread at cost, and pays no taxes. And, for fallow years to come, have I not filled the granaries by collecting from the rich—while by my hand fixed weights and measures have brought confidence to business? Further, sir, no man has found waste or ostentation in my disbursements from your treasury.

NORKID   One complaint I've never heard is that the king entertains too lavishly, or that his comptroller pays any bill too soon.

EBER   Yet even now, as we unload freight for the commonwealth, the marketplace grows silent with suspicion. Ever since you tied back the Rector's hand in favor of my office, and took his tithes for the state, poison has been percolating. In the warmest of hearts there's a cold spot for Eber and his tribe. My job is less than thankless.

GILGAMESH You've told me that virtue is its own reward. . . . But call an assembly! I'll proclaim my gratitude for the way you've civilized my laws. The announcement of my project to raise Euphrates to the level of the Tigris, and give the farmers navigation by canal, will be a good occasion to tell all Erech that it's from you I learned to plan!

EBER Please! My gracious leader—if he values my remaining service, or my life—will spare me public honors. Especially while informing the people of hydraulic engineering still in store for them.

NORKID He's all too right, sir! Don't ignite the sullen sedition in this hagridden warren of male women and female men.

GILGAMESH But even the stubble shows how good their harvests are! The grain hung heavy as peas. We've given them bread as well as walls. And when I've shown them how to feed the world, the arts will celebrate my name!

EBER Not if you don't anticipate the treachery of their slithering pope. He decries burgeoning yields as portents of famine, waterways as highroads for the enemy, and architecture as an insult to religion! He has the city festering with venom.

NORKID Any spurious flare of grievance and the simmer comes to boil!

EBER Against a spider's web, halfway measures always fail. If you don't root out that dancing-master's cult, they'll lay waste all your works the day you die—which may come sooner than necessary. Put down that bawd! Disband the College! Stamp out their rites! Pronounce an edict *now!*

GILGAMESH Am I a petty edic-tator? Let him be. This is not an ill-bred people. Let's open their eyes, not tear them out. It's not wisdom to call for force against the peace they make for love.

EBER Love! There's no love here for me and mine. The day will come when my posterity can't be saved by the memory of your power. Better that I shake this clay from my feet right now.

GILGAMESH I hold you to your word! Stay you must, a while. Without you here as my diplomatic secretary-bird, Norkid and I would have been vipered to death before our second year! I've not asked you to put fealty to me above your fear of the whirlwind God—any more than I've expected the Rector to forswear his Ishtar, or the Kassites not to pluck the dates they're offered. Remember your own words: El-Shaddai sometimes uses even Gentile means. His promise of green pastures for your seed will be kept through me because it is my promise to you to seek and grant them. Well you know also that I'd bless your sons if my offences against heaven weren't so likely to bring them curses down instead. — Meanwhile, let the city's godown reward its faithful purveyors for something more than risk at profit. Take for your own account any seven camel-loads—except lumber, stone, or arms. —Now then, bring the new copper to my furnace. Pay the Kassites with gold: it may bolster their confidence in my sagacity. —In order to avoid needless irritation, your sons will pitch their tents outside the gate.

NORKID   Sir! You're tempting providence! What's to stop them from decamping?

GILGAMESH   Have no fear. Eber will remain inside with us. From him springs all their motive, while in them lies all his hope. We have mutual hostages to our alliance. It takes all three of us friends to build up this city.

Gilgamesh goes out.

EBER   For whatever time Adonai wills that we remain in league, may we shorten the arm's length that's been between us in our past already. In the stables you will find as token of my accumulated gratitude a string of war-horses, procured by my travelers for your brave phalanx that until now has had to keep the peace on foot alone.

NORKID

[Bowing.]

On fame alone, more like. You know I have no property to offer as my thanks—beyond a certain reputation for stout alliance. Your boys can tell us if foreigners have gotten wind of the fact that we grow fewer with age, or that in my retirement from action I've become a professor of military science—specializing in parades!

EBER   With chariots you can dominate the streets.

NORKID   Come to the hall tonight. I invite all your men and mine. Beer and mutton—feasting to the limit Gilgamesh allows. I'm afraid there'll be no dancing girls.

EBER   We shall discuss harnesses, and various routes to the land of milk and honey.

Eber and Norkid go out together, laughing softly.

TABLET
TWO

[*Gilgamesh* alone in his laboratory late at night. On the back wall hangs a multiple roller of charts (as for schoolroom maps), from which a geometrical diagram of the Iso-recto-tetrahedron (IRTH) is drawn down and exposed. At first he is working at a table, occupied with the ceramic IRTH itself, drilling a hole through it, and stringing it around his neck. Off to one side is a small open-hearth furnace, anvil, buckets, and a few tools.]

GILGAMESH [Working distractedly, with frequent pauses to peer intently at the IRTH, both before and after suspending it from his neck, or to finger it as he stares into space.]

Until now every night has been a gem well spent—but this time I can't think my way. I've come up against an essence. In a rockless unwooded land I can forge these stones in a furnace—but who can make firewood? If a whole city's cooking must be done on dung and dried reeds, how can I find the fuel to bake a million bricks? I can't squeeze flame from sod! What's left to burn? There isn't heat enough in all our straw to glaze a single square-foot slab of clay.

29

Enter Lil-Amin, disheveled from sleep, standing hesitantly in a doorway. After staring around various objects she points somnambulistically to identify the drawings with the IRTH hanging on his chest.

—Lil-Amin! Without a mask! Is it you?

[*Pause.*]

At first I thought you were only a goddess. All night long divinities and I follow each other around corners as they inspect the day's damage to tradition. But you seem mortal, and here where all women are lovely there can be no doubt which one is their queen!

—Ah, my Iso-recto-tetrahedron? You weavers abhor such a lopsided signet, with too many planes but without a single facet that adds up to more or less than half a circle—especially when three out of four are only two-thirds regular.

[*Pause.*]

[He does the Dance of the IRTH, gesturing with the handle of his headless axe.]

Or perhaps it's the sharp straight lines? This tense jackstone is one corner of a cubic brick. I can hew its fundamentals with six strokes of my binary axe! With four faces of three sides each, it's the trivium and quadrivium of all faculties! It breeds all the numbers we'll ever need to count the stars or measure earth by season and degree. Even music has twelve sounds, and all words are made from twice as many.

[Seeing no response, he stops dancing.]

[*Pause.*]

But you'd rather memorize yourself to sleep with the lore you're taught than reckon by a system on your own.

LIL-AMIN
[Shaking off her trance and advancing uncertainly.]

Long ago I learned to manage sleep. But tonight fear has cut it short.

GILGAMESH   You are always safe while I am sleepless.

LIL-AMIN   Fear for Giszax himself. —I must be quick. —He has invited men to dream for him, a many-thoughted king.

GILGAMESH   But no one's done so—or dares to tell—though my cry's been out a month.

LIL-AMIN   You can force your slaves to scrape up a mountain on the river, but you can't make them dream your dreams. Since you still refuse to sleep yourself, perhaps the unbidden agency of a woman will serve your purpose.

GILGAMESH   Seeing that she's my peer, and occupies those many thoughts.

LIL-AMIN   Then listen to your dream while it's still naive, before I come to my senses and it takes the guarded lines I'll give it later.

GILGAMESH   You are right to come to me for this. Pray tell at once! Don't let your bewildered face grow thoughtful. Don't interpret, don't predict! Let me do the thinking.

LIL-AMIN

[She dances.]

Well—translated into men's language? I dreamt that I, as you, took protection of the night to learn the mystery hidden from men and unknown to foreign women. In the narthex of the Temple, I, Lil-Amin, lay uncovered in sleep as I— you, Gilgamesh—stole past without a pause. At the adytum door unvoiced words were in my ear: "No mortal man may address the hag in women's tongue." I said: "It's I, the king of Erech—only one part man, but two thirds god!"

GILGAMESH

The last time I slept, before I saw Erech, it came to me in dream that strangers somewhere were saying just those last seven words!

LIL-AMIN

[Stops dancing.]

The proof my dream is yours. But hear it out. I crept inside, toward a fissure in the earth. A crone squatted with her back to me, clawing up handfuls of wet clay to make an infant's figure, starting with the head, which hardened under her breath and had become what I took to be the featureless branch of a man that's molded for a woman's pyx. But when she smeared it with foul black tar, a flame ignited and it split along its length. Quicker than blinking, a golden serpent flashed from the shards and vanished between the lips of the cracked hollow. "Look what you've done!" she shrieked at me. "Next year there'll be no moon!" But when I bent to see her face, she smiled: and it was Inanna—Ishtar— that I saw!

GILGAMESH   You must not annotate the dream.

LIL-AMIN   Then, as you, I found myself standing high as a bird in the sky-lighted night, naked with a man's extremity, while people far below pointed arrows up at me to shoot. —Is it true that with moonlight Inanna can make a man extend himself against his will?

GILGAMESH   Expunge that dream—and all your puzzlement! I command you to wipe it clean, and forbid you to tell it to any god or person, or to remember it at all.

LIL-AMIN   I am guilty of the enigma, and doubly so to tell you.

GILGAMESH   But it's mine alone to bear. I'll take on the dread. It's not for you to ponder. I will not have its import or its expiation on any other mind.

LIL-AMIN   You have no cause to worry about my discretion—except in being here right now. They'd bury me alive. I've handed you a perfect hostage. All you have to do is tell.

GILGAMESH   Then let's study our collusion. Since you stand first in this city of arts, as artist and as living art, it's generally supposed by all that's holy we should share a bed. Yet the Widows have been heard to say you've such genius at beatitude that you have no need for atonement with a man.

LIL-AMIN   They admire mysticism, and you mistake the mockery of my solitude in that canard. It falsifies the serenity of an unanointed queen. My proper office lies vacant that was handed down from heaven. I'm sadly called the Maid of Uruk: the only one denied our priest by law—yet refused a woman's dignity by the sole pretender.

GILGAMESH   Pretender! I was scanning the world for a place to choose when your Optimates sought me out to implore my archers and my thin-lipped axe. So I delivered Ishtar's city from level carnage. But I won't propitiate her with my foreskin. I will not wear her livery just to glorify her cult!

LIL-AMIN
[With a fleeting smile.]
Now I understand a little: demigods don't sacrifice to gods!
—But who are you to scorn her mark? In return for sovereignty you swore with hands between your legs to safeguard our customs and perpetuate our rites!

GILGAMESH   They ceded me control of all destinies within the range of my bow. Do I pretend too much when I include my own? Erech's people swore to exalt whatever I exalted. Do I pretend too much when I count you among its citizens?

LIL-AMIN   Oaths of office are pronounced in ancient form and understood reasonably. Any pledge is subject to pious decency. Who would have thought ours could be taken as a mandate for your unholy pride? Instead of honoring the people's rights you edify them with bricks! Your hours of audience are filled with time-and-motion analysis. At night you try to petrify our clay by improving upon the fire of the sun; or dream up levees and ditches to reform our god-given waters! Without a plan from any god you displace a thousand households to make room for a twisted tower—and then regulate our works and days by its evil shadow! Is it fane or barrow? Tell me whether it's god's or yours!

GILGAMESH   For myself, neither castle nor hanging
[Laughing.]   garden, but an apex: to lengthen my bowshot; to look down upon the temptations of power; to give me sooner sight of your attackers; to widen my span of stars, while shortening the hours between sunset and sunrise; to

give my men a glimpse of peaks beyond the dust of your horizon; and to combine plan with profile in the perspective of my public works. For the gods, yes: a beacon for them in our middle world of seven cities. But not least for you, as sky-house for the tryst! Your canon law stipulates the highest place.

LIL-AMIN   Am I your bait to challenge heaven? Isn't the sacrilege enough—Uruk offering the Lord God Enlil a mortal bride so unperfected—without presuming to elevate her to the floor of heaven?

GILGAMESH   I do not admit that you have been wronged by me, and I mean no insult to your god. Engineering's my only art. It keeps my mind off feeling. I never felt anything before I first saw you. You are shaped to cradle me, and my thoughts yours.

LIL-AMIN   Then make your liking good. Don't remain an odious clan of one! Join the priesthood of men! Ordained, you can confirm the queen a woman, and she then consecrate you king by law. Rule no longer by default! By unnullifying me you can reduce the people's other grievances to reactionary gripes. In the end they'd praise your works forever.

[She laughs.]   Isn't that the fame you want? Circumcision is no great price to pay. It won't mutilate your faculties. Is Eber maimed? Is the Rector failing? The knife is small, and the pain is briefer than a bride's.

[He smiles.]

GILGAMESH   For you I'd suffer vultures. But no enemy's knife is small, nor the Rector's enmity so brief. But the worst of it would be to have that insolent priest heave his trophy up to Ishtar, so she could pin it to her shoulder like a bloody sleeve!

LIL-AMIN   Your pride is cowardly. If women didn't have the guts for humiliation, there'd be no one born on earth to serve the gods or you.

GILGAMESH   Still, the de-coronation is a custom I might submit to—if you'd condescend to mine. Where I come from, a king's wife doesn't play the bitch to dogs.

LIL-AMIN   Your terms are outrageous. You'd hoard the sacrament!

GILGAMESH   No, only you. If you're mine, you're not to be dispensed.

LIL-AMIN   Never have honorable guests diminished a husband's abounding riches: they magnify his glory. Besides, how could any man copy you, or steal me from you? You're the one that not even my god can dispossess. And the future woman is already yours—before sanction or touch or promise. My hand is yours; my lips, my ears, my eyes. But especially the thoughts I make up.

GILGAMESH   Yes, those feed and sleep with mine! It's they that make you the artist of your people, and in them lies my hope for apostasy. But your brain has yet to be deafened by the buzz of honey-bees. With me you'd know your gifts.

LIL-AMIN   The commonwealth comes first. Can you be prouder than the Lord Enlil? Woman's superabundance is celebrated by the gods themselves. I take on faith the catechism I teach, that even from the husband of heaven there won't be beatitude enough for the vicar of Inanna.

GILGAMESH   Mankind was given the jewel of games for you and me alone to play! My only demand is equity.

LIL-AMIN   I've heard about Northmen's equity! You'd cage me like a widowed dove, or have me follow at your heel—half forgotten when your fickle appetite is slaked.

[Softening.]   . . . though perhaps not you. I mustn't forget that you're a scandal to your own race too: a chaste barbarian!

GILGAMESH   Since I first saw you dance. Since my last sleep.

LIL-AMIN   Before your dream I had one for myself. I lay enslaved as with a blunt gleam you overshadowed me. Yet, out of shame, no beatitude would come—until Inanna, one hand resting on your back, stood smiling down at me and said: "No one can withstand him. He is now the state. You must weave his banner." Such false dreams come to me more often as my childhood lengthens. In sleep they don't seem heretical.

GILGAMESH
[Vehemently.]

To whisper that you might yield to force without offending heaven is a shabby lure! It re-reminds me that to get the peace I crave by merely spending power would be to drown like a bee in the honeyed catacomb. A rueful atonement!

LIL-AMIN
[Flaring up.]

[Scornfully.]

I despise your gloss! Didn't I say the dream was false? Who but Giszax himself has proclaimed by herald that dreams are not presentiments—only suspended speculation, pro or con? — What fatuous presumption, to say I'm provoking violence I affect to fear—in order to rob you of your strength! You're the clear free star, and I'm the deep black pool that traps you by reflection! I'm the succubus that provokes brutal lust to betray the liberty I envy! What nonsense!

GILGAMESH
[Approaching.]

I only meant that we must love each other.

LIL-AMIN   For the love of god, are you too willful
            or are you too stupid to understand
            that my renunciation of custom would
            only cheapen me to you as well as to
            my people?

GILGAMESH   Lil-Amin! This is closer than we've ever
            been before. I find I can endure the air
            you breathe!

LIL-AMIN   You abuse the confidence of a private
            dream. It's sad that frankness is a
            woman's fault, and sadder yet that a
            word, once let go, is a bird that can
            never be recaptured.

[In a lower
voice, turning
away.]
            —It sometimes happens when the moon
            is dark like this that I bewail my vows,
            and yearn to comfort as a private wife the
            only other loveless lover in all of Uruk.
            But the full will come again, and this
            lunatic will get back her wits. You can't
            corrupt me with your self-importance.

[He comes
closer.]
            —Don't touch me! —I tell you, the
            fraud is yours, to speak of passion!
            You'd scorch me with a simulation too
            tepid to keep your feet warm. I often
            wonder at the fame that preceded you
            to Uruk. The world had heard enough
            of your warp-spasm in battle—and the
            untamed generosity of your loves! But
            now here, your flaring nostrils only
            snort the steam of cogitation! Your

mighty right hand wields a stylus! Your shield-arm turns a potter's wheel! . . . For the prima donna of Uruk your liberality is sackcloth and ashes.

GILGAMESH   The liberality you want is plethora of consorts!

LIL-AMIN   Oh Queen of Heaven, who seven times inflamed all eyes in harrowed hell, I'm worth no more than a leer to our famous mountain bull! I unstring his desire with something bitter in my voice. I stink in his nose. There is no hope in me. —Must I disgrace the house of Inanna? No! Let the Rector drag the axe-man to the block! Let my people drown the Doge of Dikes in blood! —Or else myself befuddle me enough to forswear Inanna under the next onslaught of milord's residual warmth.

Lil-Amin goes off quickly.

GILGAMESH   My nights in this rimless valley have been brimming with sleepless dreams of the labyrinth beneath that brilliant heart. But she's partly right: her intelligence divides my iron blood and feeds the smithy in my head. And now her voice has given me the oracle to work on! I can use her dream without her form and substance. Let that desire wait. It won't turn rancid.

[Starts to dance, but stops abruptly.]

> —The riddle of my origin was a wraith of mist to distract me from the other idea that might have come to me in sleep!

Excitedly snatching up a bucket, *Gilgamesh runs off* another way.

TABLET THREE

[Gilgamesh's laboratory arranged for a meeting. The charts are rolled up.]

Enter Gilgamesh, wearing the IRTH, and *Eber.*

GILGAMESH
[Excited.]

I've proved it! Condensed or rarified, *pitch* will solve my problem! The bottomless bitumen that blights our swamps will bind the bricks and waterproof the walls. We'll scoop the mastic from those black puddles! We'll dip out naphtha to feed the steady flames we need for furnaces!

EBER
[Dismayed.]

You mean the tar pits? Black puddles! Bottomless pits of abomination! Stinking sludge of desolation! Burning mud is Satan's art.

GILGAMESH
[Laughing.]

Bane perhaps, but not black magic. No god would leave a miracle to me. It's by a neglected law of nature that I'll superheat my kilns!

EBER   It would be the last straw of grievances—to pollute these heathens with
the nightsoil of hell!

GILGAMESH   Their tune will change, when they
understand. It took a whole tree of cedar
logs, with my lungs for bellows, to trans-
[Indicating the   mute this pointed bit of clay. But with
IRTH.]   pitch on fire day and night, we'll petrify
all the bricks we can mold, without even
waiting for them to dry! Isn't it you
who's always warning me that God's
weather will wear away the works of sun-
dried earth? But walls all sheathed with
glittering man-made stone won't stand
to perish like our flesh; nor be worn to
dust by wind, or reduced to mud by
rain. If we can coin immortal tiles, the
future's labor will be lightened.

EBER   These laborers don't look beyond their
week.

GILGAMESH   They shall sleep while fire makes my
stone. Let them have the day in bed you
say they need every week. Take credit
for that indulgence. You'll reconcile
them yet.

EBER   Reconcile us all to Hell! Already these
sullen worms can see nothing but sarcastic pride in your monument to their
gods. If furthermore you make them
traffic with devils' dung and Satan's piss,
you'll turn them into a colony of frantic

vipers. Forever worse by far, you'll bring down the curse of Adonai on all of us! Against him an enameled tower endures no longer than a harlot's image pressed in sand. Can glossy facades repel a plague of locusts? Can the caulking of cracks keep out a rain of blood?

GILGAMESH You wanderers carry your tabernacles with you. You'll never understand the love of a fixed hearth that governs these people. Their gods call for cities.

EBER But abhor invention. You can't rub their noses in the jakes of Hell—unless you act with power and extirpate the idols that give them the courage to defy you! You've so tolerated their cult that the Rector preaches in public already! King, act on principle!

GILGAMESH I'll not be the scourge of your god any more than theirs. To you truth is so clear that it oversimplifies the web. Justice isn't economic only. You should dispense all kinds of charity. Next month the equinox will fix our common feast of feasts—the first New Year of the second polestar: the covenant that Erech will become a city of one speech, one clock, one calendar—but of all the arts. In the end my public works will earn the public's praises.

EBER

The end will be too soon if you refuse to pay attention. The public will celebrate your New Year with a vengeance. Some hokum's afoot in the temple already. Crush it in the egg!

*Enter Rector &
Optimates,*
escorted by
Norkid.

GILGAMESH

Ah, my privy council!

RECTOR
[Bowing.]

The summons from Your Lugalissimus anticipated my petition for an audience.

GILGAMESH

You know perfectly well that nobody needs a petition to see me—let alone my people's chaplain. Day and night these four doors invite unguarded. I may be stingy with holidays, but I'm generous of ear. Is your heart cowed by some anxiety?

[The Rector
hands
Gilgamesh a

RECTOR

The queen's compliments with this gift woven by her hand. A prayer rug, she declares, to bend your knee upon.

cloth. All
laugh or
smile at his
words. Gilgamesh unrolls an ensign bearing a red
and blue triskelion. With Norkid's help, he fastens it
to the wall under the rolls of charts.]

GILGAMESH

A riddle in tapestry! She knows my taste in two dimensions. I marvel at her triangular lines, woven with the perpendicular stitches of a loom! I hope her droll purpose lightened the work.

[He takes off
the IRTH
necklace and
hands it to the
Rector.]

—Here, take her as potlatch this trenchant adamantine jewel, for lack of human sculpture, to pique her interest in the third coordinate. Tell her it's a stylus for her signature in clay.

EBER
[Makes a gesture of protest.]

You're putting in his hands your tool for writing!

GILGAMESH
[Eber gives up with a shrug.]

Don't worry: I know how to make its mate. —There was a time when I got many presents from a grateful city.

RECTOR
[Motioning toward the Optimates.]

In a pinch of emergency the wise Optimates of Uruk elected to hand you the Rod and Ring. We remain indebted, even though we are obliged to oppose your innovations.

GILGAMESH   Yes, you are not enthusiastic. Your religion is too old.

RECTOR   It has not run its course. But I am no enemy of yours, as I'm told you are advised. Have I not contracted the labor for piling up our tower?

NORKID   *Our* tower! Since when, this politic change of heart?

[To Eber.]   —Why does he so suddenly clothe necessity with virtue?

EBER   He's beginning to pretend. That means they've been busier than I thought!

GILGAMESH
[Shakes hands
with each of
the Optimates.
Points to the
Triskelion.
They look at
each other.]

The right hand of peace, city fathers, grand masters of the guilds. I'd like to have your counsel in all the trades. Now that our architecture's high enough to catch the eye, it needs the skills of potters. Can you mix those colors into clay?

EBER
[Aside.]

He hopes to win over posterity with gaudy images?

RECTOR

The Optimates and I agree that all the crafts will heed your call. Furthermore, in accordance with our decision to cooperate in high ambition for the city of Inanna, we shall adjust our almanac to your equinox, keeping what we can of ancient measures handed down from heaven. It is devoutly to be hoped that my sacerdotal compromises will be forgiven—so long as we preserve the forms most dear to our people.

[Makes a
gesture of
reverence at
mention of the
goddess.]

GILGAMESH

I think you're driving at something I won't like. Let it be no tawdry sham!

OPTIMATE 1

Sir, we plead only for the way to harmonize all rites, and—

RECTOR

These gentlemen mean to say—

GILGAMESH

Let them speak.

OPTIMATE 2

—resolve all discord by a show of sacrificial contest.

RECTOR
[Hastily,
shushing up
the Optimates
by gesture.]

As mathematician I have come to see the reason in your duodecimal scheme. By calculation I still could fix the dates for planting. But when it dawns on people that after this New Year you'll be abolishing the month of Epact, which Enlil gave them with their city when time began, sooner or later—

NORKID

I'm sure you'll see that it's sooner.

RECTOR

—there'll be riot, and the end to all my management. Unless you act right now.

GILGAMESH

Every year they'll have a five-day feast. More frequent revelry. No long wait for reelections! Every blessed year your calendar will be true to Sun. It's *he* that makes Euphrates rise. You should pray accordingly.

RECTOR

None old enough to swing a scythe will forget the thirteenth moon given Inanna by Father Enlil. The people are maddened enough by a bachelor for king. But strife and tumult won't serve the gods. The temple thrives on peace—and the temple is the state.

GILGAMESH

What act are you implanting in my stateless will?

RECTOR First, withhold your intercalary decree until this New Year has begun. It's time enough when the people have tired of their pleasures—after you have pleased them most by winning the Rod and Ring from their champion. Your power to alter the city's tradition will be recognized and cheered if he has been worthy of the queen before you strike him down.

GILGAMESH I told you that I want no puppet putting me to the test. I won't abuse your law with play-acting. Otherwise, I agree in advance to any suitor you put forward.

[Eber and Norkid express consternation.]

RECTOR Of course I speak of nothing more than the king's reinauguration. It's the rite of Epact that rids us of our sins.

[To Eber.]

[To Gilgamesh.]

—During the feast you will lie hidden in undiminished royalty, like a god withdrawn, while the Lord of Misrule struts and boasts. Finally, when the braggart's purple is stained with dissipation, you'll recapitulate your fame by cutting short the mockery.

GILGAMESH Fatuity I suppose will awaken my bloodlust to simply kill the pretender who's trying to kill me first. But I warn you that I'll not accept for sake of protocol some innocent fool deceived by adulation. I won't murder a puppy.

NORKID   Gilgamesh, don't tempt fate! Better make-believe than real surprise: treachery in the trappings of their ceremony!

RECTOR   A decent stranger, so elated by a few days of royal emoluments and perquisites that he'll fight to keep them.

EBER   Make him tell you who's his pick already!

RECTOR   My Temple hunters, tracking lions up into Aram on the rivers, venturing beyond the sight of smoke from hearth or altar, have happened upon the wild man known to legend as Enkidu.

NORKID   Engidu! By mere chance, eh? Just stumbled on him! It must have been a right cool search, beating all the bushes of Akkady. By accident you enlist the abominable windman—who abhors the faintest whiff of featherless bipeds!

EBER   This explains the gossip that's been showing up in my reports! That horned and hairy monster lives with the beasts, speaks their lore, and judges all their cases.

GILGAMESH   I've heard tales of Engidu, but never to believe. He instructs lions, outruns the cheetah, and protects the oryx.

RECTOR   Full of the hot red life that gods and mortals love to smell. Blood-power well to be expended. No danger to you of course in a duel of human skill. But to capture him will take more force than the Temple has.

GILGAMESH   I myself will fetch him!

RECTOR &   Absolutely forbidden! —Not the king!
OPTIMATES   —Against all religion! —It would defeat the purpose! [etc.]

NORKID   Without you on hand we couldn't keep the people at work for even three
[Aside to   days!
Gilgamesh.]

EBER   It's conspiracy, playing upon your lesser
[Aside to   pride!
Gilgamesh.]

GILGAMESH   I forgot. —You go, Norkid. —And rev-
[Grinning at   erend sir, you must go with him, as
the Rector,   spokesman for the law. I promise that
who hesitates   Eber will not usurp your crosier. —The
and then bows   name of Engidu is something to bite
with icy   on. Fast as a javelin and hard as an axe.
formality.]   Is it true that he can uproot an oak in anger? —With the Rector out of town, I can spare a few of your men. Pick volunteers who aren't half-cocked string-happy heroes. Take the battle-net. Bring in Engidu fresh and unscathed.

NORKID   I'm the very understudy of Gilgamesh himself, but how in the name of Mazda am I expected to snare alive some troglodytic aborigine of superhuman senses living at the end of a rainbow in league with all the fauna? I'll have to crease him with an arrow first.

RECTOR   The victim must not be either pained or drugged!

GILGAMESH   Then use the surest lure. Take the woman with you.

ALL   —Who? —What woman? —What do you mean? [etc.]

GILGAMESH   Lil-Amin.

OPTIMATES   The queen! She can't leave the Temple.
[Their dismay   —An insult to Inanna! —She won't go
is first shared   outside the walls!
by the Rector,
who soon bethinks himself however, making the
effort to conceal his unexpected satisfaction.]

GILGAMESH   I so decree. No further discussion. Engidu may hate mankind, but she'll have an opposite affect. Have her open up her robe. Let the dog sniff. Soon enough he'll have to share the scent with gods and packs of saints— after he fells old Gilgamesh! You may catch them in the net together.

EBER   With open eyes you walk right into the trap of this hoodwinking whoremonger!

RECTOR
[Blandly spreading his palms.]

It's not I that offered the queen. My hands are clean. They toil for love.

GILGAMESH
Aside to *Eber and Norkid,* taking them by the elbow as *he and they slowly walk off,* while the Rector keeps his Opimates quiet.

Eber, my old friend, there are times when one quick stroke should cut the knot. With both of them absent from their altar, there'll be no one here to stampede the herd before I can top off the present work. —You see, I'm sufficiently suspicious. —Norkid, don't let the Rector outnumber you with his glebe-men: no more than two or three as guides. Any trouble, I trust you to keep it diplomatic. . . .

OPTIMATE 1

Let Your Grace put a stop to this sacrilege! You hardly lift your hand!

OPTIMATE 2

Call out the mob tonight! We'll die before we let her go!

RECTOR
[Soothing them.]

No, there's no summons to waste your death. The catastrophe is his. Suddenly an old oracle is about to be understood.

OPTIMATE 2

The gods will turn on us in unison if Lil-Amin is allowed to be dragged into the wilderness and ravaged by a bestial foundling!

OPTIMATE 1

Who will ever stop the whims of this sleepless mountain bull—if our pontiff gives him leave to paw the dust?

RECTOR
[Turning on them impatiently.]

Fools! It's not for laymen to interpret prodigies, or to judge the evil destined for a good to follow. Your piety dwells too much on custom. The fall of Gilgamesh will be accomplished if we endure the last vicissitude of his regime. I tell you the Tablets of Fate are about to be fulfilled. Find no fault with my tolerance of this expedition. It's I, Our Lady's dancer, who has suffered most; and it's I, the lawkeeper, who will bring down the law upon this tyrant. And when the glebe's restored, we shall possess his miscalculated monument as the city's bond to heaven! It is the will of the gods that for us Gilgamesh should raise this ladder up to heaven! . . . On a nuptial dais in the firmament, my sister's frankincense and myrrh will smell all the sweeter to Our Lord.

[Strides back and forth, here and there breaking into dance.]

OPTIMATE 1   We defer to you in matters of divinity even when no precedent is found. But will Engidu reduce our taxes?

OPTIMATE 2   In any case, how can we be sure he'll win the Rod and Ring? People whisper that Gilgamesh is two-thirds god.

RECTOR   Two thirds can't save the mortal part! Engidu is sent to us by Inanna. When he's seen there'll be no doubt of the issue. We can rest assured he's quicker and stronger by half than the stories claim. Gilgamesh won't get the chance to dance.

OPTIMATE 2

Then we should prime the people to welcome their redeemer. Old women will grow young with expectation!

RECTOR
[Dancing by way of illustration.]

[Leaving off his dance.]

No! Rejoicing must be contained in the mummery. Let the jubilation seem sarcastic. "The King of Beasts" they may acclaim him, decked in purple, riding backwards on his ass. —That interloping vizier never ceases to probe the pus of hatred swelling in my liver. His spies and provocateurs are still to be feared. If he incites the northmen to forestall us, you'll die with feathers sticking out of your lungs. But may Tigris join Euphrates if I don't scatter his bones— and stamp out all his children like isolated ants!

OPTIMATES
[Chanting in antiphony, perhaps with dance.]

—Exalted shall be the sacred fool who laughs when we mock him :: that he may leap for the hand at our throat!
—Happy shall be the King of the Epact :: to sow his seed like stars of the sky!
—Blessed shall be the lion of the steppes :: for he lays low the raging mountain bull!

Optimates go out.

RECTOR

[Inspecting Gilgamesh's laboratory, idly pulling down various rollers, but pausing at the three-dimensional diagram of the IRTH, which he still holds in his hand. At the end he suddenly unrolls and hangs up a banner displaying the blue five-point star.]

Now I must convince the virgin queen that Enlil's law is broad enough to sanction such reversal. Gilgamesh shall never have her! Engidu is no lover for her heart: let him open the unstitched seam that's forbidden to her brother and confessor. When she's our mistress at last, she'll learn the worth of her one true minister.   —Meanwhile let her scorn this gage. What an absurd talisman: Iso-Recto-Tetrahedron!   —The fourth facet wouldn't be so bad if it weren't the shape that makes a star of Eber. Yet soon we'll be bowing again to the lovely star of Inanna! —Salt, indeed! By the good Lord, I'll salt his tears!

The Rector leaves, following Optimates.

TABLET FOUR

Gilgamesh and Eber enter the Laboratory by torchlight.

[During the conversation with Eber, Gilgamesh unrolls a series of the charts, thereby covering the tapestry affixed by the Rector in Tablet Three. Some of the charts he merely glances at; others he studies with varying degrees of attention: a site plan of the city, drawings of the ziggurat (tower), a flow-chart of the construction project, and projective geometrical drawings of the IRTH.]

GILGAMESH   All works take longer than they should. So my motto is: predict too soon, and finish soon enough. Production is at last improving. The building trades have learned to heed my specifications. Work-orders regulate their habits.

EBER   It's an army under lash. You might as easily push them into war as force their arts and crafts.

GILGAMESH   You must admit bitumen was a good idea. Not for a moment has fuel been lacking. Watertight pitch makes hellish heat—as well as perpetual torches to light more work at night! In the flames aloft, when there's no moon, the new tiles gleam like sapphire, lapis lazuli, and rubied copper. By that heap of beacons I dare the thunderbolts to find me after dark!

EBER   You think their gods will be dazzled by ersatz stones in girlish colors? Leaving only Engidu for you to fight? Shall I tie one hand behind your back?

GILGAMESH   Without sarcasm now, tell me what you think: does he abhor my works? Or will they fill him with delight? I wonder if he's really ugly.

EBER   These beauty-lovers want him in your place regardless. A man who lies with beasts should be stoned outside the gates, instead of welcomed like a bridegroom! But the women have gone out to greet him with garlands already! Are you going to let a stupid game of force bring all your works to desolation?

GILGAMESH   No man exists with greater strength than mine.

EBER   But an animal may be faster and more cunning. —Still, all things are reported to me, and I'll ferret out his weakness. It's possible that by some device we can survive him.

GILGAMESH   Not by trickery!

EBER   The trick is to forestall the Rector's tricks. No longer can my vigilance alone keep the chain-mail of his conspiracy unmeshed. Yet you send Norkid on a hospitality expedition!

GILGAMESH   Your wariness has not been wasted. Had not your One True God set his face against my enemies, no doubt I'd long since have fallen to poison or my own unreckoning. But I don't want to keep the Rod and Ring on Shaddai's sufferance!

EBER   You abuse His gift of will by thwarting His favor with stiffnecked caprice. But it's not as prophet that I protest your negligence. By your command I'm responsible for the body politic. Furthermore, daughters of Erech now bear my children's seed. Therefore allow me to ward off my own destruction by urging you against your pride. A great spirit gets time to grow still greater if it's less magnanimous about the way to stay alive in single combat.

GILGAMESH	There'd be no greatness of any kind in consenting to a secret handicap. If I deserve my power and my life, I must contest the categories of life and power. It's the law of nature that spirit be sustained by gross faculties of body.
Norkid enters, travel-worn and weary.	—Is Engidu intact? What about the priest-woman? Did you have to push her? How long did it take? How did she—
NORKID [Smiling wryly.]	Good my lord, I'm not strolling back from an idle bout of chess. Give me leave to catch my breath—and savor your joy at seeing me again. I'm happy to find that you too are still alive.
GILGAMESH [Grinning, reaches Norkid a mug.]	Hello, old dogface! —Your beer's been waiting. —I hear you've landed the prince of the peaceable kingdom. — What have we here? A puny bow!
NORKID [Hands Gilgamesh the bow of a fire-drill.]	His present to you. The scepter he rules by. For making fires when you're all alone. Her Highness had given him your Iso-recto-tetrahedron.
GILGAMESH	That was the lure that did it?
NORKID	I couldn't say what did it.
GILGAMESH [Examining the bow.]	I'll tighten the string and play it pizzicato while I wait for New Year's Day; or pass the time like a bard, thrumming deeds I've never done.

NORKID
[Drinking deep.]

She called it her one private jewel. But she also gave him another, as we would have said back home. The goddess favors Engidu, and everyone knows it. You can smell incense in the street.

EBER

That gorilla will have the mob on his side before the feast even begins. You should have kept him out of sight.

NORKID
[Gilgamesh lays down the drill and takes up his axe, which has been remounted with its double head.]

Of course I brought him in as a hooded prisoner after dark; but how do you disguise such a specimen? A swarm of honeybees was waiting at the gate! When this pretender's all adorned with gold and purple, and led before the people with their queen, it will take thunder and lightning to reduce him to a scapegoat!

EBER

The Rector's busy transmogrifying bees to hornets.

NORKID

[Gilgamesh hurls his axe into the floor, where it remains sticking.]

In his mind it's all over but the acclamation. He began to taste the restoration as soon as he saw his royal sister about to be disburdened of her natural imperfection by a holy savage already incised with the barb of religion—congenital proof of Ishtar's choice! At two hundred yards Engidu's notch was as prominent as the Rector's miter. Maybe he was born ithyphallic too, because until he was relieved of his superabundance, it looked as if he was goose-stepping on the run!

[*Pause.*]

Being the clairvoyant hound of Gilgamesh, I bristled with presentiment—the
sparrow's horror at a sudden shadow on
the sun. You should have seen the ferocity of him before she sheared his mane
and dressed his loins! Without the lady's
help, I'd rather have tried to lasso a
crazed elephant!

GILGAMESH   If you'd killed him I would have pardoned you.

NORKID   So lightly you now disclaim the threat
that frightened me the most! Still, I
tried to disobey my orders. Nearly in a
palsy, I fitted a silver-tipped arrow to
my bow. It's not easy to aim at the son
of a goddess when your nerves are shaking like a cornered rabbit's. He hadn't
seen us, but he heard the shaft, caught
it in his hand, and flung it back at me
like a javelin, but twice as fast. Thank
god it must have been deflected by the
volley I'd ordered in my panic. Twice,
with our Rector's shrieks splitting the
silence of high noon, we skirred a band
of sky. But Engidu stepped among the
arrows as if they were children stream-
ing out to play. It was eerie: no shadow,
no echo, no engagement!
—The guides broke cover and ran. One
of them he got on the back of the head
with his bannerstone, thrown by the

[Dances, or
slightly mimes,
dry and
sporadic
illustrations of
his story.]

handle. The other two he overtook in easy bounds, and spilled their brains by banging the two skulls together.

GILGAMESH   I'm glad you missed. Your blind devotion would have disgraced me.

NORKID   Or cost you my worthless life. What saved me and mine was his awe of the lady. It made him see that he was naked. He retired to the hills, escorted by the animals that had been at the water hole. Next day, nevertheless, he returned in the same condition—still shy. But not as timid as the hares and gazelles and foxes and wolves and lions. Like us, they hung back to watch the unveiling from a distance.

[Gilgamesh retrieves his axe and hones it with a whetstone.]

[Norkid sits down to drink pensively.]

GILGAMESH   What unveiling?

EBER   Unveiling of a whore! How much distance?

NORKID   We couldn't see much from our side of the grove, and His Grace nearly had a conniption when she refused to take him along as master of ceremonies. But I reckon there's not much doubt about the consummation. Three days later she led Engidu out through the trees clothed like you and wearing the Iso-recto-tetrahedron. The animals had fled, and he was no more innocent than she who was laughing at his familiarities.

GILGAMESH   What familiarities?

NORKID   That's all there is to tell. After that wedding he was brought here for all the feastings of a potentate. The rest is detail.

GILGAMESH   Detail is what you're paid for, captain!
[Flaring up.]   Details are all I want. A general needs no report on net results. Did she dance?

NORKID   The Rector seemed to visualize what we couldn't see of her courtship. He was skirling on that weird pipe of his—a thin monotony; it stood my hair on end, and would have swayed a cobra on its haunches: the only sound for twenty miles. Then his music stopped—an officious cue for her Cry of the Maidenhead. It finally came, like a fainting afterthought.

GILGAMESH   What courage, to have danced in her very terror!

NORKID   That's your imagination of a Gilgamissy girl! Engidu has no horns and he isn't ugly. If she trembled, 'twas not in fright. She was prepared for her duty!

[Gilgamesh
fiddles with
the bow,
using one
GILGAMESH   You mistook her poise. I think she
of Norkid's   stood with frozen veins, dreading to be
arrows as a   seized. Those shudders are invisible.
fire-drill.]

NORKID   All right. I'm no psychologist. But she opened up her robe.

GILGAMESH   As she'd been instructed. But she didn't make advances.

NORKID   I didn't say he was backward. Knee to knee, he didn't need a schoolmarm's prompting.

GILGAMESH [Raising his voice.]   Norkid, were they like dogs, blinded by instinct?

NORKID   Dogs don't make love when they couple. Or talk. He had speech to learn. She taught him how to use his tongue.

GILGAMESH   It's natural he'd love her. But the converse doesn't hold. She has no use for a troglodyte.

NORKID   I'm not a spy—my job was to bring the victim back alive—but I could see she wasn't too proud to let her eyes be opened. It was no surprise that an imaginative spinster, roused by priestcraft, should fall for an adoring gallant who wishes to deliver her from a fate worse than death.

GILGAMESH   But then he grabbed her brutally. It was too rough and quick. He was incorrigible and rude, probably quite smelly.

NORKID   You seem to think that woman's as fastidious as a white raven. Haven't you noticed the way she walks? For her the unwashed ruffian was a princely changeling. On the way home he was in her tent at every bivouac, and in the morning she was always starry-eyed. You could almost hear the purring. As we traveled she would smile and close her eyes, rehearsing all the stitches she had taken.

GILGAMESH
[Angrily.]   Why didn't you just rope the fellow and carry him here trussed upsidedown on a pole—without all those hornpipe solemnities?

NORKID   Sooner than be tied he would've gnawed off all four paws. Possibly you'll kill him yet, but I wish I'd done it before she brought him sorrow. In putting on the new man he gave up the old. He lost a dozen tongues by licking hers. Old littermates no longer listen to his calls.

EBER   A fool's exchange. He's no smart trader. If his lust can't be slaked in one white sepulcher, there's still a whole catacomb of hot sarcophagi stewing for his marrow. Before an ordeal, whoring cannot help him. A savage isn't bred for urban stamina.

NORKID

[Polishing his spectacles.]

False hope, my friend. Even when he beclouded with beer the grief of being shunned by his animals, the honeymoon did not bereave him of strength or speed. Dissipation is his tonic, and funeral his resurrection. One sundown we camped on the edge of the steppes near some village that was terrorized by a rogue lion he had tamed. The shepherds came to ask his help. So by my leave he set out to tell the beast about mankind's sheep-laws. But dragging off another ewe between its teeth, it ignored his warning. In an amazed fury he threw off his clothes, grabbed the lion, and in half a minute tore the life out of it with his bare hands. When the frenzy left him, and he saw that he had killed, he carried the carcass to Lil-Amin, twice his own weight, asking her what to make of murder. As tender education of Engidu's ferocity, all night long they waked the poor lion. But in the morning, as usual, nothing drunk or done by himself or the woman had softened him up.

GILGAMESH   Did you say he sometimes sleeps?

NORKID   As much as a cat—as much or as little. Sleeps and leaps indifferently. By the pain of guilt he earned the praise that men reserve for a mighty hunter. He began to play the lion's part as our provider. Like a big carnivorous cat he found he also relished other blood. The blood of prey that used to flock to him for safety.

GILGAMESH   So he's aching for the thrill of more momentous sacrifice!

NORKID   The priest harped on that theme in his religious instruction: expiation of his kills by killing for the gods, to save their people, and win the Rod and Ring from the raging mountain bull who oppresses the numberless women of Ishtar's city and all her livestock. Meanwhile of course to me the Rector affects to be duping a victim too ignorant to suspect that the famous skill of Gilgamesh will be backed by the sacred force of custom. Of course I never left them alone together. You should make that a rule as long as you live.

GILGAMESH   Let the schemer proselytize. What difference does it make? Conspiracy's too linguistic for an aboriginal ear.

EBER   But that harlot's in the plot. How does she ply the golem's remorse?

NORKID   Their pillow-talk was not for ears of mine. All I know is that he battens on tales of Gilgamesh. He who never saw a wall now envisions himself commanding a tower. He who never saw a rite now imagines splendid liturgies in Gilgamesh's raiment. He who never heard of gods now calls himself the champion of Inanna.

GILGAMESH   Yet from inborn slavery to her the poor fish doesn't know his lack of air!

NORKID   But fighting man-to-man that fish won't feel out of water. Don't count on having time to size him up. He won't wait for you to start it.

GILGAMESH   If the first move gives an edge, why then he and I will strike at the same

Plucking on the fire-bow, Gilgamesh picks up his axe and goes off.

time. But he will feed the immortal maggots. I'll play the dirge while women mourn his mortal parts.

NORKID   By bruising his widow's spikenard Engidu has merely unlocked her perfume for our royal anchorite. She's not one to lose her fragrance at the center like a wornout cake of soap. It seems Gilgamesh is about to learn that such virtue renews itself in the giving.

EBER   The three of us could be dead already! I'll watch the ayatollah. You watch the ape.

Eber and Norkid walk off together.

TABLET
FIVE

[Before dawn on the day before New Year's. The temple sacristy to stage left of a dividing wall; stairs of the tower to the right. The sacristy is identified by the five-point star motif on a short screen (which makes an el with the wall) concealing Lil-Amin's bath; a loom is visible upstage. A sacrifice has just been celebrated, and the under-priestesses (Widows) are returning from the temple to the sound of recessional music from within. The ritual style is penitential.]

Lil-Amin enters, masked and in eucharistic vestments, *preceded by Widows.*

[In ceremonial but perfunctory fashion, during the following dialogue, they relieve her of a bloody knife on its sacred plate, and divest her one by one of tiara, chasuble, stole, maniple, cincture, amice, and alb (or mimed suggestions thereof). She herself may touch nothing. It is given to understand that other Widows are meanwhile passing back and forth with jars of water and hot stones. Finally they remove her mask and shift as she steps into her lustral bath out of sight. At first she appears dazed, praying by rote and exchanging formal bows with her acolytes.]

LIL-AMIN

Oh nuns of Inanna, blessed is the Queen of Heaven.
Oh ye servants of the Father Enlil, praise him forever.
Oh holy sisters, walk in the ways of Our Lady,
and glorify the prince of gods. Magnify the Lord.

WIDOWS

Amen.

LIL-AMIN
[Kneels, facing the temple.]

O Lord Enlil, who has suffered me to minister this day in your holy temple, mercifully pardon the faults of my service, and vouchsafe to grant that on the highest altar of my people in the night to come I may receive without blemish the grace of your loins, and make myself acceptable to you as the vicar of Inanna in her own city here on earth, who lives and reigns your heavenly daughter in the world without end.

WIDOWS

Amen.

LIL-AMIN
[Rises. The Widows undress her and prepare the bath as she gradually recovers.]

All those years as a girl I dreaded my first sacrifice. It's strange how cool I was with the knife. I didn't fall faint with pity when the blood splattered my skin. Instead, I took pleasure in my style, and felt nothing for the throbbing sow as I slit her belly open that might well have lived to farrow many more. The embryos still quivered. I thought how painless breeding is, for boars.

[She steps behind the screen.]

—Sisters, help me cleanse this female blood.

WIDOW 1   The cauls were perfect in the womb!

WIDOW 2   Your blood-voice was clear and strong.
[They bathe her behind the screen.]
Your penitential dance was flawless. Surely it's now forgiven, your journey beyond the scan of Uruk. Heaven knows it was to right seven long years of wrong.

LIL-AMIN   My new worthiness is small. Dawn's air still smells of famine. The moon is dark and the sun is loathe to rise. It goes hard for me so to please heaven's bridegroom that he will stay the Great Gods' Council, to keep the waters from coming to an end. I, the one most weak and terrified in all this city, not yet learned even in the ways of men, must feign the supremacy of sacred desire! I tremble more as victim than I did as hunter.

WIDOW 2   Your trembling brought on beatitude. Enlil's heart will be gladdened by earth's most holy bride. He will trace the shape of your skin, and love's tide will rise in his golden thigh.

LIL-AMIN   It will be the plowing of a salted field. My liver's shriveled and my heart benumbed. I am dead before I climb those stairs. The god will cinder me with lightning.

WIDOW 1   Yet your spirit lives, like barley-seed in a moistened grave! A withered ear of grain is sevenfold reborn.

WIDOW 2   In tonight's vigil you'll learn your way by prayer, meditating the hopes you uphold of all Uruk:

WIDOWS

[Widows dance.]

—that the cow of the field will yet be covered by the bull.

—that man will no longer turn from woman.

—no bride ever again sit in grief beside her bed.

Gilgamesh appears, invisible to them, coming down the stairs outside the sacristy wall. [He carries Engidu's fire-bow,

—For the fragrance of your sanctity will be giddy musk to the king of gods in his nostril.

—For the counsel will prevail of soft-eyed Inanna in the Chamber of the Gods.

—And Enkidu will wrest from Giszax the Rod and Ring of her own city.

LIL-AMIN

moving without purpose until he catches the sound of their voices. Then puts his ear to the wall, as if

Now I'm clean. —Go sweep the sanctuary. —You go dress the meat. —Then come back with the herbs and unguents. The queen of Uruk must be doctored as she's passed from male to male like a bruised heifer until she calves. I know nothing of the mystery I to the opening of an air-duct, straining to hear.] *Widows go off* into the temple. [Lil-Amin remains behind the screen. Gilgamesh strikes a single note on the bow, which gives her pause; but she continues.

. . .

He then plucks two notes. Another pause and continuation.

. . .

Finally he sounds three notes.]

profess. In all good faith, how can I deceive Our Lord when I'm stiff and cold from collarbone to ankle? They say a god is manly, and cannot fail to want me. Enkidu said that even when scared I could draw oaks down from the hills by their roots! Yet I myself am no better than the ghost of a hollow dried-up tree, my honey petrified. . . . It's the people that I fear for most. I pity them who put their trust in me. There's no health for them in a sick-hearted queen. . . . But sweet Inanna, pity *me*—doomed by birth to be your servant! Was I a changeling? It's harder for me to walk up those steps and open my robe to the divine guardian of our race than it was for you to harrow all hell naked! I'll have no strength in me when I reach the top. Keep me at least from screaming. Let me faint on the Lord's bed, and avert my face, before the bolt of glory shatters this lump of half-baked clay. Does it pierce like flame, or spear? —What's that? . . . Who's there? . . . You must not come into the sacristy!

GILGAMESH   It's me.

LIL-AMIN   Enkidu? Not here! Not now! Go back, go back!

GILGAMESH
[Hesitating.]   I, Gilgamesh, with the string of Engidu.

LIL-AMIN

Oh no! No, no, no! They'll annihilate you here!

GILGAMESH
[Gaily.]

Deep calls to deep! Thought to thought! Eye to eye! Ear to ear! Tongue to tongue! Pelt to pelt!

LIL-AMIN

[*Pause.*]

You mean stone to wool. Furnace to loom. Tar to holy water. Sleepless prowling to the sleep of love.

GILGAMESH

Then tree to root! Or sun to moon!

LIL-AMIN
[With a short laugh.]

Twain that meet in eclipse.

GILGAMESH

Are you naked?

LIL-AMIN

I wear no jewels.

GILGAMESH

You gave away mine.

LIL-AMIN

To buy that music-stick for you who had sent me!

GILGAMESH

To me you never reported your success.

LIL-AMIN
Widows enter, preceded by horizontally carried flabellums, which they solemnly wave at her. Then dropping the fans, *they go out* again.

Was it likely that I'd fail?
—Shisss! Someone's coming.
—Be careful! Don't touch me! —Now go sprinkle the Veil of Inanna with seawater from the Apsu well. But first take care to inspect it thread by thread. Give it a blessing when you take it out of the tabernacle, and again at the door, with balsam. Try to walk with dignity.

[Lil-Amin resumes in a whisper.]

—Go away, Giszax! You have enemies enough, without calling down the wrath of our Father in Heaven.

[*Silence.*]

Are you still there?

[*Silence.*]

Can you hear me? —There's no way of getting in here without being seen by the Widows. Dear God, I pray he hasn't killed them!

[In sudden fear she reaches out from behind the screen and snatches up one of the fans by its head. The long handle is seen probing vaguely in self-defense.]

GILGAMESH   I haven't changed. I'm still no beast of prey. I still don't sack my cities.

LIL-AMIN   It's I who have changed.

GILGAMESH   You cannot be less fine.

LIL-AMIN   From the worm you saw I've become a butterfly. As an old maid at the loom my knowledge was imagined, my speech too idle. But I no longer waste.

GILGAMESH   You were Ishtar's artist. And day by day you still increase in worth. I look forward to your wrinkles.

LIL-AMIN   You've waited too long in the looking. I do what is decreed above our heads. Your fate too will be inscribed tomorrow.

GILGAMESH
[Laughs.]

Perhaps I shall be obliged to alter one of those decisions. Or change your office. But you are a tree of innumerable harvests, which blossoms at fruition. My wedding present bears neither fruit nor flowers, but I have topped it off with Zagros evergreen. I molded the last brick, fired the last tile, pointed the last course with my own bitumen. The whole Sea-Land and all its seven cities look to the mountain I have made for your featherbed of bliss.

LIL-AMIN

As the destined platform for our Lord High God's descent to earth, it's an afterthought of your willed obsession.

GILGAMESH

It was my will to reconsider everything for you. I'm steersman, not a rudder. The afterthought is heaven's. Let my tower serve for all your marriages.

LIL-AMIN

Why do you come to taunt me, Giszax? It was not by my choice that I seemed fair to an impetuous champion. He had never seen a hairless face.

GILGAMESH

Or thigh. What was it made you dance against your will? I'm told he didn't have to lift your skirt. Did he lick your salty palm?

LIL-AMIN

It was the will of Inanna that spirit stood aside for body.

GILGAMESH

It's said your spirit was radiant.

LIL-AMIN   Are you here to spite my radiance?

GILGAMESH   I am here by chance. Is it true that by taking Engidu you left the peaceable kingdom in a snarl?

LIL-AMIN   The orders came from you, the duty from Inanna. I did not go with joy. But desire roused cannot be flouted.

GILGAMESH   Unless it's mine, apparently.

LIL-AMIN   You vaunt your sovereignty of mind! Ha! —I tell you, for myself and him it was Inanna who enkindled motive.

GILGAMESH   Then disobey the gods that use you! Stop Ishtar's game!

LIL-AMIN   The game of Inanna is the work of life.

GILGAMESH   So it was the means of work that made you love him?

LIL-AMIN   The means were ends. His chest pressed against mine. I did the work of a woman. It wasn't love. No, it was not love—at first.

GILGAMESH   At first! Then when did it begin? Were you in love a minute later?

LIL-AMIN   For pity's sake, it's like asking life itself when life began to ask me what I felt or when! At times he and I were halves of a single dancer—one breathing out, the other breathing in. Is that what you call love?

GILGAMESH   One tidbit of a mouse and you purr like a lion's mate.

LIL-AMIN   Oh he was gentle, but never mousy!

GILGAMESH   Mouse or lion, he'll die before he has the chance to roar!

Widows enter, singing.

WIDOWS   *Softly run Euphrates*
[They carry a blue veil behind the screen, where   *Until we end this song.*
The veil of Inanna
For Enlil's night on earth.

LIL-AMIN   My mother once wore this. —Mind you don't touch me! —There. Now carry up linen from the cedar chest, and make up the bed exactly as the Rector showed you. Our Lord's mask goes up late in the afternoon, with the flowers. Don't forget the bridesmaid's prayer when you finish.

they dress Lil-Amin, who then appears from behind the screen in a blue diaphanous gown, her own mask in hand. One of the

WIDOWS   *Softly run Euphrates*
Widows sprinkles her with an aspergillum.]   *Until we end this song.*

Widows go off, crossing downstage to the opposite side. [They carry various objects up the stairs. Shielding their eyes against the bright daylight outside the wall, they barely miss Gilgamesh, who manages to shrink back unseen. Lil-Amin listens, at first with a frown.]

LIL-AMIN	Giszax?
GILGAMESH [Lil-Amin smiles to herself.]	Here am I. How tractable you are—with cats and gods: anyone but me!
LIL-AMIN	You sent me to the cat. You raised my bed to God. You and my brother agreed to it all.
GILGAMESH	I allow for your religion. When both the circumcised transients are gone, the question between us will remain.
LIL-AMIN	Enlil's bride can never be a private wife!
GILGAMESH [He starts forward	I don't agree to that.
LIL-AMIN around the projecting el, slowly groping his way through a dark and unknown passage.	It's a pity you won't be consulted. Tomorrow before dawn, behind the double doors, the Council of Gods will cast the New Year's lots: every person's, mine, and yours. Your two-thirds of a vote won't be solicited.
GILGAMESH He speaks progressively louder as he	As plenipotentiary for myself, I act without instructions. So can you. For us, you and I decide!

moves away from the mouth of the ventilation duct (so that she may not suspect his change of position); her voice sounds commensurately fainter. As he rounds the el and approaches her, he lowers his voice, and hers sounds louder, until they are again in equilibrium.]

LIL-AMIN   What can we decide? To flee? To live in the marsh weaving nets for fish and making love for brats? You can decide to build a hut with reeds! . . . Did your mother have no gods, that you're immune to retribution? Not Enkidu, but you, should play the King of Fools!

GILGAMESH   Do you pray for him to kill me?

LIL-AMIN   Can you expect the sympathy of Inanna's high priestess?

GILGAMESH   But the private person, what does she hope?

LIL-AMIN   The private person drifts without hope, the orphan of Uruk, beyond the river's mother-reach, like an empty coracle at sea. Let wind and tide decree her course without entreaty. How can a floater be sure of what she wants, alone in the shoreless night without a moon? But I know that if you kill Enkidu, black cancer will eat away the sun, and miasmic naphtha rot away the bindings of our bones. The Optimates would arraign my feebleness, and the Rector would condemn his own sister for the city's failure to lift its curse. If Enkidu dies, I die too!

GILGAMESH   Not under my protection!

LIL-AMIN   They'd have ways to kill me. Unless you did so first.

GILGAMESH   Why would I kill my heart's desire?

LIL-AMIN   For keeping her vows. For remaining unbeholden to your weak preference. Her autonomy would enrage you. A tyrant can't endure paradox.

GILGAMESH   My exclusive preference is preeminently strong. What's more, being deeper, more contented than loose servitude to mother nature. It's your match too— when I have the only wife for me in all four quarters of the universe.

LIL-AMIN   Even after Enkidu? And after tonight? I thought you said—

GILGAMESH   Even after circumcision! *After* anything perhaps. But not *before* any subsequent dancer! No successor while I live.

LIL-AMIN   The mighty Nimrod has used me for his decoy, and now he wants jealous title to my carcass!

GILGAMESH   If I were master you'd be mistress.

LIL-AMIN   The symmetry is false. Equality isn't equity for a woman. You'd level our atonement, limiting my beatitude to yours!

GILGAMESH   There's no limit to the mind. I speak of Gilgamesh and Lil-Amin, not of man and woman!

LIL-AMIN

As if keeping the caste at two were as hard on you as me! A dog in the manger that wants a bitch as brood stock. To be reduced to your chattel is for me no honor. But you have never honored the ways of kings, and none that come after will ever honor yours.

GILGAMESH

[He is now so close to her, without detection, that

But Engidu wasn't raised by women either. He's been king of kings in the bush. Not the man to esteem himself too little, once he grasps the Rod and Ring.

LIL-AMIN

he must deflect his voice with one hand to his mouth.

Wrong! He's sensitive to gender, with an inner ear for rhythms, studious of the dual dance. When you're dead I'll teach him more. He's adept at patience.

GILGAMESH
She turns to the dividing wall, puzzled

Before his patience sleeps, your dancing panther will bite the dust of one who takes no sedatives!

LIL-AMIN

by his altered tones.]

He's kind to me, and as intelligent as a sister in knowing what will please. But if he ever palters with my sovereignty, I can finish him off with my inexhaustible allures!

[She laughs.]

GILGAMESH
[He steps up behind her. At the sound of his voice she spins around and shrinks

You're already thin to the bone from overwork! But I thank him for ravishing the arrested beauty of your pucelage. In your face now is what I'd hoped to see! Though I suppose you've also been fasting.

LIL-AMIN
back in fear, but
immediately
recovers from her
surprise.]

Holy Mother, I thought you sounded much too close! You can't come in here!

GILGAMESH

Who's not a cat may look at a queen. This is the place for a fly on the wall! I see that a woman's mystery battens on her penance.

LIL-AMIN
[He takes a
step toward
her.]

There's no mystery about women in a female city. —Don't come near me! I refuse to become your accessory!

GILGAMESH
[Smiling.]

You lured me here with your existence.

LIL-AMIN

Get out of here! I'm not fascinated.

GILGAMESH

When I am gone—

LIL-AMIN
[Turning
away.]

—there'll be no one to praise me for my thoughts. Gilgamesh is but once. When he is gone, it will be as if the cruel sun went out. To rid my office of his begrudging glare I must lose the light I see by, and deprive the city of blazing invention. —Yet I promise you I'll put aside the loom and ply the fire-craft you've taught us. I'll use any art that serves my way to perpetuate your works. I need Enkidu to loosen up the law, but no consort shall repossess your seat, or occupy your cot. Why should the people of a woman-god have any king at all? *I'll* build the seven walls! *I'll* erect seven towers for the seven cities of seven gods!

[Facing him
again.]

GILGAMESH
[Laughing at her.]

If I'd only known you cared for power! I'd've long since handed you the plans and got some sleep.

LIL-AMIN
[She dreamily mimics his characteristic acts and gestures, as they might seem to a child. At which he laughs happily.]

To become an actress, I've studied all your acts. Before your huge eyes are closed, I mean to take in all their vision. I know how to draw plans and issue specifications; by anatomizing space, to control the use of time; to appraise skills and apportion tasks; to examine small movements and seek innocent causes of untoward effects; to be friendly and aloof; to bend and stiffen. I can imitate your face, and how you walk, and even how you swing your axe. My method will put your moods to use.

GILGAMESH

You're a keen student, but you can't inherit your teacher's memory. Design is also made of details; and it takes the particulars of experience to realize plans through gangs of men. It will take somewhat closer acquaintance to acquire all my lore. Therefore let me live another seven years, and help you learn much more!

LIL-AMIN

I already know more than you think. I make everyone tell me versions of your criticisms. I've sent reporters north for stories of your past. Taking up mathematics and ceramics, I've analyzed the Iso-recto-tetrahedron by its syllables. I

[Lil-Amin performs her version of the dance of the IRTH.]

can dance your theorem of squared tri-angles. I don't know the proof, of course, but the fourth face is perfect, with long and equal sides, each of which when squared is equal to one third the full cube's surface. —The rest I get by experiment. See: the condensation of your battle-cry, the acorn of your oak!

GILGAMESH But you didn't keep the clay-stone I gave you.

LIL-AMIN I only pawned it. I'll have it back as souvenir. But you see, I've memorized your theme. By my resonance you'll live in fame.

GILGAMESH Then you must resonate my desire now. Project my sleepless hope. Show the craving that scrapes my unglazed clay.

[Her dance changes to reflect his words.]

Dance the turbulence of this aquifer that undermines my roots. But don't just counterfeit the harmonics of two joined rivers, or of two spines touching, opposite but like, where four legs meet!

LIL-AMIN I can immortalize your vibrations with-out your mortal power, but it's not for the sounding board to propagate your seed.

GILGAMESH [Thoughtfully.] You seem too sure that I'm the one will die. Does the Rector intend to daub Engidu's fingernails with venom?

LIL-AMIN   No necessity for that. Would I be memorializing you if there were any hope? Giszax isn't equal to a lion with human hands and superhuman motion.

GILGAMESH   Better warn him too, if you're an expert in the manly art! You can't blame me for opposing the gods in self-defense.

LIL-AMIN   And when, before you know it, you're emptied of your blood, all breath spent, your disconceited ghost can't blame me I if don't suppress the cheers. The mask of power will staunch my wound and smooth the flux of pain. My widow breasts will harden before the milk begins to well. Tight-lipped I'll beat my chest, subjugate my brother, and set free pigheaded will against all varieties of wisdom—my heart commemorating yours in wanton purity of pride!

GILGAMESH   I didn't suck my strength from milk, and I won't die to favor a necromancing witch!

LIL-AMIN   So after all it's fear that keeps you from me! Fear, fear, fear! You're afraid of what I am, and call it mystery! —Oh Blessed Lady Inanna, pardon my consideration of the secondary sex. Giszax can go to hell—body, shade, and name!

Carrying her mask, *Lil-Amin runs off* into the temple. *Gilgamesh,* giving pause to his astonishment, *walks off* the other way.

TABLET SIX

[Morning of New Year's Eve. A space outside the temple, with tower stairs as before. Stage left, the great double doors to the council hall of the gods are now dominant. A pair of three-legged royal seats stands upstage, the one to the left occupied by Enlil's Council Mask. The Traders and their interlocutors take foreground (downstage) positions such that the ceremonies behind them are continuously seen but only sometimes heard.]

Eber and the Traders enter, carrying their shepherd crooks and the Troopers' bows.

EBER	Their gods have been carried into the Chamber of Destinies already, so now it's all right to watch; but give those doors a wide berth. —Keep those bows out of sight! But I don't think our friends will call for them at such close quarters. — After the coronation you can go celebrate New Year's. When fixed and
[The Traders lay down the bows.]	

movable day are the same, it's a feast of reconciliation. Let Gilgamesh call it the sun-god's. At least the foolishness is shortened to twenty-four hours.

[The doors open slowly from within.]

TRADER I

Widows, Lil-Amin, Optimates, & Rector enter, in procession. [Lil-Amin is dressed as a masked bride.

Father, my heart's as anxious as any native's to hear the messenger hail this new moon, for I fear the vengeance of the God of the World. By speaking slyly, according to your light, you have accepted the shah's unholy calendar.

EBER

The Widows, as bridesmaids, beat a rhythm with pestle-cymbals. The Rector carries a heavy crosier, with which he controls the ceremonies by thumping upon the floor. The Optimates close and seal the double doors, while Lil-Amin is led to take her seat on the right. They all touch their foreheads to the ground in front of Enlil's empty mask before moving to their places in the

Even from angels the will of Shaddai is often hidden. . . . I am not faultless maybe. It's a narrow line I tread. By opposing superstition I strengthen blasphemy. But the king has yielded to my policies, as these heathens have yielded to his demand for hell-oil. I can only hope to keep the peace while we wait for God's word to reveal itself day by day.

RECTOR

ensuing ritual. The Rector intones his walking homily with perfunctory forrmality.]

The gods asked one another, and chose Enlil to lead their decisions; for when chaos was full he had saved them from the dragon. With four currents of wind he hewed from earth and water a land of plenty between the two great rivers on their course to the sea; and set the black-haired people to attend with sacrifices bountiful and savory the seven lovely houses of the gods; and first among them was the city of his daughter Inanna. But we have allowed ourselves to be led into grievous strife with her law. We have menaced her altar with evil. Once again our manifold wickedness has disordered the spirit of Uruk. In our weakness we have failed to hold fast the love of our sacred mother. The serene and gracious moon has been taken from our sky, and the pitiless sun means to drink the river from our fields. Our bread is turned to stone. May Enlil look with mercy upon the the servants of Inanna, the despair of her heart! —Bring the old king before the seat of god to

Gilgamesh enters from the right, escorted by Troopers. [He wears a horned crown on his mask,

confess his transgressions. —May the gods renew this kingship by fatal decree, and grant their people another year of life. . . .

and carries the Rod and Ring. The Troopers bear the Triskelion banner as a gonfalon. Leaving Gilgamesh near the Rector at center, they take up positions opposite the Traders downstage, who speak to each other in the foreground. Eber moves as close

TRADER 2

as possible to Gilgamesh without interfering in the ritual.]

They bring in their year by offering their choicest harlot on the highest place they've got. If she doesn't pacify the overlord idol, comes fire and brimstone!

TRADER 1   Law to them is nothing. Each year beforehand, divine consent to chance is chiseled as their destiny! All their piety goes toward learning how to guess the future. Righteousness does not avail.

TRADER 2   The Name of the One God, world without end.

OPTIMATES   *His word looms a stormcloud on the horizon.*

WIDOWS   *Amen.*

TRADER 2   Gilgamesh insisted on going through this. I hope our father can keep him from doing something rash. It would wrong our unborn seed to die for a Gentile. But the Troopers don't expect a crisis yet. Tonight they'll be carousing. Having been born in snow, they exalt the sun.

TRADER 1   Thank God this is the year of zero epact. With calendars in conjunction, we can agree for the moment with both kinds of heathen! For us the pleasure of acquiescence is all too rare.

[Upstage ritual action continues separately, its music and chanted words merely suggested, except where emerging into the text.]

TRADER 2   I don't see how the holidays are going to be so pleasant if the people don't get any friendlier.

[The Widows and Optimates perform

TRADER 1
elements of restrained dance.]

These are the days they serve their servants and have their scapegoat lead the revels! They'll welcome circumcised foreigners.

TRADER 2

I'd like to be happy in Erech. Why should we abhor the stationary arts and comforts? I didn't ask for levitical responsibility. It's not my idea to be against these women. In the middle of a dance who can ponder law?

TRADER 1

The famous guest-cup is not for us, and orgy is forbidden.

TRADER 2

No other nation is tested by self-abnegation!

RECTOR

. . . Confess the insubordination of your rule.

GILGAMESH
[He satisfies ceremonial form and tone ironically, affecting to pretend that his semantic substitutions are as traditional as the coronation itself.]

I confess that none of my designs has been handed down from heaven. No god has envisioned my plans or approved them. I have taken it upon myself to make new things and devise more efficacious ways. By me the polity has been reformed, and idle artisans put to new inventions. In drastic supervision, never have I closed my ear or turned a blind eye. Worst of all, I have altered fate by refusing Ishtar's brand, and eschewing her adulterations. If these be offences to Enlil, then do I admit them.

OPTIMATES   *Amen.*
[The Widows
titter at their
slow wits.]

TRADER 2   Gilgamesh is right to hold with a man's fatherhood.

RECTOR   . . . As Lugal of Uruk, say what you have done to serve her.

GILGAMESH   I have given Enlil a ladder down to earth, and the whole Sea-Land a beacon for caravans and boats. It flashes blue sunbeams into the deep of the sky, and its shadow walks across the city to cool the heads of children.

TRADER 2   They lure their god with a doctrine of incest.

RECTOR   For trafficking in vile mire, may you be spared the wrath of Enlil; for polluting our city with the smoke of slime.

GILGAMESH   Incense and orisons vanish like a mist;
[The Rector   even hecatombs are not prolonged: but
removes   my freewill offering of fired earth winds
Gilgamesh's   an upward path that will endure for all
mask rather   our gods. Neither can it be pulled down
abruptly and   by armies nor scattered by thunder.
lays it on
Enlil's seat.]

TRADER 2   Only battered to an ant hill by the four winds of El-Shaddai!

RECTOR

[Gilgamesh solemnly hands the Rod and Ring to Lil-Amin, but mockingly bows his face to the ground before her seat instead of Enlil's.]

Yield up the Rod and Ring, and await the proof by custom, that you may contend to rule. Bow to the throne of Enlil. Until the king returns, let a stranger bear the retribution!

[*Thumps once with his crosier.*]

Hark: I hear a knocking!

[*Silence. . . . Thumps twice.*]

Who knocks for kingship?

[*Silence. . . . Thumps three times.*]

Engidu enters, escorted by Norkid.
[Optimates conduct Engidu to the Rector. Norkid

Enter, Lord of the Epact. . . . Do you swear to serve Uruk, and for love of Inanna carry from her streets the sins of long dark night?

ENGIDU

goes to stand with his men. Engidu looks at Gilgamesh.]

Do I.

[*Sneezes.*]

Smell feathers make me cough.

RECTOR

[He rips off Gilgamesh's cloak (leaving him as bare as a slave), who starts to react but checks himself. The Rector then slaps Gilgamesh's face, somewhat harder than protocol requires. This time the latter responds with an open offer of violence—at which the Rector does not flinch. The troopers lay hand to swords, but

Relinquish the purple!

[*Aside to Gilgamesh:*] Sir, we beg your public indulgence of our tradition immemorial.

—Lead the dying king to solitude. Let him eat dust and quench his thirst with penance. —We must break his pride!

[*Thumps repeatedly in a drumming beat.*]

TRADER 2   No salt tears from that prince of men!
Norkid   Contrition, never!
stops them with
a gesture. Eber restrains Gilgamesh with a touch.
The Rector smiles at him, bowing ironically, and
resumes with ritual intonation.

RECTOR   Banish this uncircumcised barbarian
from the eyes of gods!
The Optimates awkwardly fling a net over
Gilgamesh. He remains calm but uneasy, staring back
at Engidu, who has been fascinated by him.]

OPTIMATES &   —You have all day to put a stop to time,
WIDOWS   your Royal Lugalissimus! —Halt the sun
[Ad lib in   with arrows! —Piss up Euphrates; make
various voices,   him flow to the mountains! —Forbid
jeering. They
taunt him in   the moon to grow! —Draft the masons
sing-song and   to wall out Engidu! —Save your neck by
with bits of   axioms! Prove the theorem that Giszax's
mocking
dance.]   more than half immortal! —Cauterize
your wounds with salt. Glaze out the
dew on your eyeballs! —We'll smoke
your carcass with stink-fire, and embalm
it with bitumen!

TRADER 2   Tiny minds uncork their genius.

OPTIMATES &   —Cogitate your freedom, Oh Philoso-
WIDOWS   pher-King! Reckon away those knots.
—Find that battle-axe of yours! Hack
your way out of the butterfly net! —
Giszax, Giszax, time to go berserk!
Show us the rage that your hillbillies
thought was so awesome! Let's hear the
battle-cry that weakened the knees of
mountain ewes! —Bring down the

temple with your Lifo-righto-textile-
peed-on! —Oh savior of the city,
invent yourself salvation! —After your
parts are strewn around the brickyard,
you'll be glad enough to share the
favors of a female grave with local dogs!

TRADER 2   Son of the Nephilim, is there an angel to
save you from this humiliation? Instead
of mocking the savage, they turn their
scorn on you!

RECTOR   Enough. [*Thumps patiently.*] Enough.
[Smiling.]

WIDOWS   —Before you go, sir alchemist, answer us
our riddle: what's two-thirds hydrogen
plus one-third oxygen but can't get
through a fish net?

TRADER 1   Gilgamesh is a son of man. If he falls, he
falls.

TRADER 2   And down we go with him!

OPTIMATES   —Yes, go hide in your kiln, where
Enkidu can't find you!

Gilgamesh   —Soak yourself in creosote and fire up
saunters off,   your guts!
draped in the
net. [They make
a show of kicking him out. Animated by their own
bravery, they snatch the Triskelion gonfalon from
the Troopers, who thereupon draw their swords.
The Traders move to the rescue with suddenly
revealed short-swords in one hand and their
formidable crooks in the other. Norkid wades in
with bare hands to make peace among them, while
one of the Optimates tries to trample the
Triskelion. Another Optimate gives a little scream.]
Gilgamesh re-enters, at another point, to watch
unseen.

RECTOR   Order! Order! [*Thumping in earnest.*] Let it stay!

WIDOWS
[Calling after Gilgamesh, as they think.]

—Yes, harden your codpiece with glaze! —Go play with your Erecto-testro-gilga-heathen! —Don't look here for any straightlaced nanny-goat that doesn't know the world is made for horny billies!

LIL-AMIN
[With dignity. Commotion ceases. The Triskelion is restored.]

Silence! Silence for the coronation! For shame, on Enlil's wedding feast! Nor will the new king be any better pleased. —Rector, give me peace, or clear the court!

NORKID
[Adjusting his spectacles. Troopers and Traders deploy to positions of control.]

I will, if he does not. While I'm alive, he won't turn temple mummery into a coup d'etat!

[*A moment of silence.*]

RECTOR   Temporarily we submit to force. There'll be no holy war if the principal trial takes place according to the law.

EBER   The law is Gilgamesh. We can extirpate your priestcraft.

RECTOR   I deign to answer houseless nomads and rabid fascists only with my opinion that the bull which goeth before the herd is but a cattle like those that follow.

NORKID

[Troopers and Traders slowly return to their former places.]

Sufficient unto the day is the anxiety thereof. That's this fascist's motto. But if Gilgamesh won't deign to scotch the snakes that hatch before our eyes, I have no such compunction. Thinking of the future I've been known to forget my orders.

RECTOR   Captain, you are an honorable soldier!

NORKID   My tongue has no bones, and wags as it will. An occupational compensation for our mindless rote. —Men, *as you* WERE!

LIL-AMIN   Let the rite proceed.

[Ceremony resumes.

TROOPER 1   My sword-palm itches to churn some flesh. Gilgamesh is not here now to protect the owners of our rightful spoils.

Troopers and Traders converse with

TROOPER 2   There's no use in plunder if you can't take it with you. And it's better to hack your way home after a feast than slay your host before he serves the eats! No one's going to be poisoned if we make the ayatollah taste it first.

each other in the foreground. Behind them the Rector invests Engidu with Gilgamesh's mantle. In

TRADER 2   What about us? We're dead already! This swarm of drones covets our imported goods. They also want the daughters back that were given us for wives by the erstwhile liberator who confiscated their temple treasury to pay for a pile of bricks! It doesn't make them hate us the less that he, our only defender, has surrendered to their folklore. The chief idolater is no priest of reconciliation!

dumbshow: Engidu, while still bewildered by civilization, prompted by the Rector, accepts the Rod and Ring from Lil-Amin; he is then led to the empty throne

TROOPER 2
[beside her and
crowned with
Gilgamesh's
mask.]

Be of good cheer. Gilgamesh hasn't lost
his nerve. He studies dreams too much,
and for the moment some kingdom in
his head seems more important; but our
troubles fade as Mithra's fire climbs the
zodiac.

ENGIDU
[Speaks shyly
and haltingly
what he's tried
to memorize.]

Oh Lady-Amin, highmost priest, and
Op-timates of Ur-ek. Oh great womens
and man, many as sands. I have shaking
de gates at my arm. Soon wid hand I
break ark-enemy on eart' of In-an-anna.

WIDOWS
[Chanting in
dance.]

As earlier with human hands
You unset human snares for beasts,
And then for humans laid the lion low,
Deliver us from evil now.

RECTOR
[Touches
Engidu's head
with blood
from Lil-
Amin's
sacrificial dish.]

I anoint Enkidu, Imperator of the Epact,
to try his strength against Gilgamesh;
and if he fails the verdict to perish in his
stead. —Take up kingship of the feast, to
command us as you will, until you lose
or win the place you sit in!

ENGIDU
[Speaks
haltingly but
with gradually
gained
confidence.]

Do I what speak you. I ready be for old
bull of able-value blood! One life from
two will blow away on wind. I kill him
to lady-god and cover-god. Me city-king
all years will be.

WIDOWS

Women and men, raise your joyful cry:
Eu-oi, Eu-oi!

RECTOR &
WIDOWS

Sleep not, until the New Year cracks its
shell.

[Intoned as antiphonal litany.]

—Lest Enlil frown upon the black-haired folk in everlasting night. Sleep not, until the night's dark lid begins to open, until you see the slitted eye of light.

—Lest his bridal bed be made a nesting place for vultures. Sleep not, until you hark a voice from the east with tidings of the silver crescent.

—Lest the house of our gods be filled with dust and leveled like a desert tomb.

—Lest the merciless sun cake dry all mud with cracks, and choke with sand the living waters.

—Lest time go on without return.

WIDOWS   *Give ear for word of Inanna her sky-boat! Watch for the horns of her bullock!*

TROOPER 2   It's not the moon that sprouts beer-barley; so how can she inaugurate a year? They don't understand the constant mill of time. Mithra lingers and retreats, but he never wanes!

RECTOR   When on high the gods chose Enlil to weave all destinies . . .

TRADER 2   The harlot they call a queen, she wasn't good enough for a blasphemous king, but for them she's pure messiah!

TROOPER 1   You patriarchals should have more respect for ladies of the cloth. She's the finest kind. Have you ever seen her dance? Or have you lost the yen, what with all your wives?

TROOPER 2   Nobody but Gilgamesh would refuse to touch the one woman anywhere that's his own true match.

TROOPER 1   But the perfect bride from folk to god, for god to folk!

WIDOWS   — . . . a pious bride.
[They lead Lil-Amin down from her throne, removing her mask and robes, leaving her dressed only in the blue bridal veil.]

—May our full, perfect, and living sacrifice be gladly received by her mystic bridegroom; and her beatitude bring upon us gifts of God. Let us make communion by the light of stars, in the shadow of Our Lord on her skin.
By the first sweet gleam of moon
Enlil greets his lovely bride!

RECTOR   Weep not for garments, milady, when the lord of gods has gently plucked this knotted cord. Your gleaming skin will adorn the incensed linen like a cloven pearl. In the fearless manner of desire, like the petals of a lily, you must receive the savior of us all. Then shall you be reclothed in tender caresses, and dressed in Enlil's misty salt-sweet breath. His sea-soft hand will gently warm your bud-tipped breast. You shall feel his kiss on your lips. He will come unto you with lifted glory; your knees shall be parted by his golden ivory thigh. . . .
[Kneeling before her, he loops a white cord three times about her waist and ties it lightly. His ritual prayer gradually grows more personal in address. Everyone falls silent as his voice lowers. Breaking off, he kisses her feet passionately.]

—Oh my sister Lil-Amin! Lil-Amin! The rapture of your god is forbidden to your priest! In every other sacrifice I have proved that I grudge great Enlil nothing

I can have or know, nor life itself. But I give him you in anguish! I forebode the levin by which a god may infuse the beatitude that women dare not dream of. I dread that he will utterly consume you! Why should earth's jealous father release from divine atonement the most precious daughter of mankind, and restore to me the life that illuminates my humble altar? For me of all men it is most unlawful to serve as his attorney at love. He does not favor the testimony of my unhallowed desire. —I cannot follow you to heaven; yet I am the solicitor of Uruk, and thus, as lawyer to you, the city's proxy, though before a bar too high for human counsel, I arraign our accursed warlord's tower for raising your bridal bed too high!

[The Urukians stir uneasily.]

[The Widows lead her to the tower stairs. The Rector remains on his knees.]

Slowly *Lil-Amin disappears* up the stairs. [The *Widows return,* dancing accompaniment to the Rector's private prayer, and come to a stand between Troopers and Traders.]

TROOPER 2   Thus spake the all-too-human pope! This Messpot duty still unfolds a few surprises.

ENGIDU   She love me! Peoples love me! I love allbody!
[He shouts and smiles spontaneously, growing more and more excited, to the amusement of everyone except the Rector, who arises and turns away to recover himself.]

TRADER 2   Thus spake orangutan!

OPTIMATE 1   Our ox is jealous of the Lord!
[Amazed.]

WIDOWS

[They dance. Little by little everybody's solemnity yields to merriment and the rite dissolves into general festivity.]

—Listen for the sighs of fathers!

—Hearken to the songs of young husbands!

—Guess the yearnings of blood-stirred boys!
Open the hearts of women!

—The bull will lift his head in the pasture,

—and the cow will lift her tail:
when Lil-Amin makes Enlil love!

—Journeymen will be set loose like cowboys

—to lift the skirts of wedded girls
when Lil-Amin makes love in the sky!

—Seven thousand times seven are the bids that await seven thousand wives baking folds of soft white bread. Pray not to waste a single drop of pearly yeast!
Swim swiftly, sweet Euphrates,
Until we end this dance!

—Merrily, merrily, merrily,

—Do not lose the chance!

RECTOR

[Smiling and genial, signaling the end of formality.]

[Engidu lays the Gilgamesh mask on the seat and puts the Ring of

[Thumps heartily.]

Yes, dear guests of Uruk, it's not for you to watch this wedding in solemn silence. Strangers, welcome! Citizens, rejoice! Your choice of meat: wild boar killed by Engidu without a wound; or succulent lamb well drained of blood, to suit those that bring us salt. Custom is suspended! Let innocence drown all *office on his head like a rakish garland, handling the Rod like a swagger stick.]*

wisdom. Eat, drink, and dance: for the world may end tomorrow! —Your Highness, lead us to the end of time!

OPTIMATE I   Ask your whim, Engidu the First! Rule thou our disorder!

ENGIDU   Is all woman the same?

OPTIMATE I
Optimates go off with Engidu, capering.

Does not each stick make its own smoke?

RECTOR
[To Eber, gesturing cordial invitation.]

May it please Your Honor and his distinguished sons! Our banquet is afforded by the economy you teach us. General welfare offends no god.

EBER   I have made no pact, Your Grace.

RECTOR   Our humble gratitude entails no obligation to the guest. On holiday we shed all cares of office.

NORKID   Come along, Eb! There's nothing wrong with a truce. It can't hurt to help warm up the fun-king. As long as we're cold sober before it's over.

EBER
[Bowing to the Rector.]

Then my thanks already for your hospitality pro tem.

NORKID
[Taking them both by the arm.]

As long as our Gilgamesh remains the autocrat ontologically.

RECTOR   I've always admired your vocabulary.

NORKID   It comes from cosmopolitan occupa-
Norkid, Rector,   tions. Take us to the belly-dancers.
and Eber go off
smiling at each
other.

WIDOW 2   You could do worse than take your
[To Traders.]   father's hint.

TROOPER 1   You called us some goddam awful
names.

WIDOW 1   I did think the best part of you ran down
your mother's leg.

TROOPER 1   Maybe we could be rehabilitated.

WIDOW 1   With some beer we could discuss your
therapy.

TROOPER 1   Yes, Ma'am!
*Troopers dash
off.*

WIDOW 1   This is the dance of rising sap.

[Widows
mimic a

WIDOW 2   For the palm to bear dates, seed must
belly-dance.]   find its way to her flower.

WIDOW 1   I'm more for sap than seed. But these
tame Traders are famous for their fructi-
fications.

TRADER 1   I'm so well married, I thought it would
take a devil to make me wicked. But I
must admit your torso is savory to my
eye already.

WIDOW 2   Your eyes are nice. But we're not pictures. Our temple is not that kind of museum.

TRADER 2   Would you like to hear some tent music?

Troopers return,
TROOPER 1   First we wet our whistles. Let's all suck
each with a jug   the fennel stalk.
and long straw.

WIDOW 2   A toast to the fifth and final sense!

[A Widow, a
TROOPER 2   Drink to the supreme sacrifice!

Trader, and a
TROOPER 1   If it's sacrifice, who wants to live forever?

Trooper take turns
at each straw.]

TRADER 2   Of course it's a small thing to want a woman.

TROOPER 1   For me it's a small thing after I get what I want.

WIDOW 2   But not for long, I hope. You should
[Traders   consult a specialist.
dance.]

WIDOW 1   According to the whispers of our exogamous sisters, we may have more to learn than teach from these educated sheiks.

WIDOW 2   They're charming when they make us sheep's eyes, but I lean toward military
[Pointing to   men. —That northman now, that wrin-
Trooper 2.]   kles up his nose every time he lets an
[Troopers get   arrow fly: I always like to watch him
up to do a   shoot.
sword dance.

WIDOW 1

[Widows keep sipping as they produce dainty food. Traders and Troopers eat morsels.]

On their feet, both these types have pros and cons. Judging just by song and dance, until they meet the test, let's award a bouquet of fig blossoms to all these handsome guests.

TROOPER 2   Praise be to Ishtar that it's not a prize of cherries!

WIDOW 2   I'll separate rams from billygoats by the way they bite and chew my seedcakes.

WIDOW 1   For my part, gentlemen, draw straws.

. . .

[*A Trooper and a Trader draw from different jugs.*]

[She claps with glee.]

There's nothing to choose between them! They deserve equal entertainment. Praise be to Mithra and Shaddai both, we're neither maids nor wives! Let no one rise from this feast unsatisfied! The night's as long as the day!

[Throwing aside the straws, they

WIDOW 2

take turns drinking from

TROOPER 2

the jugs, on the fly, Troopers,

WIDOW 1

Widows, and Traders dancing in a ring.]

But not long enough. Somebody ask Giszax to hold back the sun!

Not today he wouldn't! Don't forget his sexy-jismal system and zero impact!

A stitch in the bush saves nine in time. I didn't take the veil for contemplation and celestial studies!

TRADERS   —Brethren and sisteren, it's useless to be shrewd!
—Mingle rhymes that blow like the wind!

WIDOWS   *No wight who dares complain or frown*
Will be allowed to lift my gown!

TRADERS   *There's almost nothing half so sweet*
As your exotic heaps of wheat!

TROOPERS   *When we finish all these beers*
We'll quit the corps of engineers!

WIDOW 2   Behold, I shall climb into the highest palm tree and take hold of all its branches.

Widows, Troopers, and Traders snake-dance off to the banquet. *Gilgamesh* crosses to the opposite side, walking backward to look after them with amusement, and *disappears.*

TABLET
SEVEN

[The middle of the night. Same scene as Tablet Six except that the royal seats are replaced by a kettledrum. Its drumstick leans against the wall.]

Gilgamesh enters, carrying his mounted axe in one hand and the Rector's crosier in the other. [Goes directly up to the double doors and addresses them.]

GILGAMESH [*Knocks politely with the head of the crosier.*]
Gods, this is Gilgamesh whose name must be pronounced before you engrave the contingent fates of others. I'd like to speak to you, please.
[*Silence. Knocks again.*]

Admit me to your man-made chamber. I wish to make a suggestion. Listen to me. Take a recess, while Enlil absents himself to consummate the city's marriage. Spare yourselves the trouble of casting lots on our behalf. Dice were

113

made for pure amusement. Wasn't it the very purpose of creating mortals to provide yourselves with leisure?

[To audience.]

(When the world was young they had to till their own fields and build their own houses. They had no art. The seven cities of Sumer were founded as slave quarters. The walls were made of mud. They should be grateful that I've improved their plantation.)

[To doors.]

Can you hear me?

[*Silence. He knocks again, vehemently.*]

The Tablets of Fate are much too long. You could briefly decree our destiny in gross. Why bother with the warps and woofs? No need to endure a tedious night wrangling out the details. Reduce your New Year prescriptions to a few terse gnomes. If other people did as I have done, they'd tell their own story as they went along, day by day, and write the verses for you.

[*Silence again. He knocks less vigorously.*]

Listen, you all: my predecessors here were no more than priests or judges, but I have organized the kind of army you never dreamed of, in your imperial service. Where else has your lugal built a port to heaven? I'm entitled to the courtesy of a little conversation. Even if the riddle means I'm neither god nor man, but stand alone between, I should be

[He examines the doors minutely, feeling with his fingers, vainly seeking entrance.]

consulted at your caucus as the engineer of your own public works.

[*Silence. He sounds the drum with his palm.*]

Doors, why do you keep me from the parliament? Open, or I'll break in upon my relatives!

[To audience.] (I should be welcome. They'll never find themselves another such producer. But now, on seven thrones carved from stone and carried here by human beings, the gods deny me audience! I have over-estimated their gratitude to the species they like to make love to. Yet there's more imagination in the wits of any weaver's apprentice or halfbaked potter than in all these sagacious mollycoddled majesties. They have the privilege of inscribing those Tablets merely because they happened to come first and live for-ever. By no other virtue do they ordain the world's history, which we should wrest from destiny when their fingers are loosened at this hiatus of time. It's solely owing to the damned eternity of gods that herds and populations must wait for them to propound the next twelve months. But they should know that for me it's worse than living by chance alone to have chance's part predestined. See how anxiously they bar their ozoned hall when epact-time opens a crack in their firmament!)

[To doors.]

I concede weather and conception for you to fix at random, but we the people should determine what and when to do.

[*He strikes the drum with the crosier. Silence.*]

Just imagine you hadn't called this meeting: Would the seasons have run amok or merged, or men and women felt alike? Would there have been an end to daylight? No insemination of the dates or sprouting of the barley? I think

[Dropping the crosier, he drives his axe through the drum skin. He then throws the axe at the doors, where it sticks by the blade. He retrieves the axe and unsuccessfully pries with its blade at the cracks of the doorway.]

not. You've concealed from your servants their freehold! It's sorry bosses who fear the competence of workers! You've ruled your drones by infixing self-fulfilled prophecies. —I've been a hypocrite to mute my contempt for your control of every hour of the year. What is fate in fact but history abstracted—the gods' intention ex post facto! Anyone who survives me can claim to have prescribed whatever it turns out I will have done. But if Enlil finds it necessary to disintegrate me for sacrilege, then he must confess that last year's Fate has failed!

[To audience.]

(Still, if it's nevertheless somehow true they spin and snip all my years, the hour to act is NOW!)

[To doors, which make no sound as he pounds on them with his bare fist. He then chops at them with his axe, in increasing fury, but to no effect.

Doors of cedar, I know well enough why you stop me! If I interrupt the assembly before new fates are fixed, we'll have our liberty by default! Skittish gods, twitch your ears in consternation! Oh pusillanimous absolutes, eagles cowering in your covert like rabbits! Affect languid indifference if you like, but let me in to kiss your feet! . . . Unless you've simply levanted, and left me besieging an empty garrison!

Throwing down the axe, he snatches up the crosier and, using both hands, beats on the dull doors with the flat of its crook. The crosier breaks in two. He flings away the pieces and starts for the stairs.]

—Oh my god, has Enlil left already? — Then I'll race him to the bride! The ladder down from heaven is there for me to climb! On the feast of feasts I'll break my fast, and live like Engidu by nature! Ah, that deep sweet slippage of the touch, rooting for the flower underground! I'll butter his bun!—unless he beats me to it. Or join the dance, if it's already begun. But what if I find him mounted, undulating naked as a winged snake? He'd better take cover in the upper air—or spend a thunderbolt on me!

Engidu enters, decked in the purple mantle and wearing the IRTH, but tired and discouraged, carrying the Rod and Ring negligently in one hand, his bannerstone (an axe-like weapon) in the other.

[He sniffs the air, sneezes, and only then sees Gilgamesh. Dropping everything, he leaps for the shoulders just as Gilgamesh hears him and whirls around to face him. Engidu misses his grasp and ends up on the stairs above Gilgamesh, looking down upon him.]

—The circumcised wild man! I forgot about *your* fate! We meet again too soon.

ENGIDU

[He notices the broken crosier

Smell feathers before see you! Not go up there. No man do that! You know?

GILGAMESH

and comes down past Gilgamesh to

Is Ishtar's lion here to defend her lamb? You're a pretty crafty son of a bitch to sneak up on me like that.

ENGIDU

pick up the two pieces.]

Stick from temple magic-man. You kill my friend, brother from Lady-Amin!

GILGAMESH

Great friend: bring poor hagridden stripling to die in woman-cage! You ate acorns and ran with gazelles. A friend would not have brought you to a city's mockery.

ENGIDU

[He menaces Gilgamesh in the attitude of

People need me kill you later. But you go on tower, I kill you now! New king guard queen from bad bull.

GILGAMESH

a rampant lion, who only turns away and goes down front. Engidu mistakes the move for a retreat and follows aggressively; yet when Gilgamesh

Maybe the only reason I'll be killing you instead is that when I was young I studied the wisdom in an old man's way of fighting, before I needed it to win. Furthermore, you'll be crapulous with meat and beer. You who were suckled by lions have slain your milk-brothers and eaten the flesh that alive consoled you. Now

suddenly turns
to face him, as
if to take his
arm, he
momentarily
shrinks from
contact.]

you're lured by the fame of a women's bazaar. But they haven't told you how terrible it is to face my battle-warp. Norkid says red clouds gather at my head and the air around me glows. Go back to your real friends, now that you know how women taste. I'll open the gate and let you out—right now, before they miss you.

ENGIDU No! All people love me, hate you.

GILGAMESH It's galling to be disputed by a foundling creature, misguided into vice, swaggering at a woman's apron string, strutting in front of lily-livered caterers. Go back to the steppes, where strife and love are

[Roused by
what he takes

artless, brother ape.

ENGIDU Two times called me monkey, kinfolk I

to be an insult,
Engidu casts off
his mantle and
springs to attack.

like not. Ugh! Other day I killed king of animals. Now kill you!

Gilgamesh readily joins the fight, which is like a dance punctuated by the lightning movements of real combat. Gilgamesh is the boxer, avoiding Engidu's grasping blows with a sophisticated guard and precise footwork while annoying him with light jabs. At first Engidu fights like a baffled wrestler, as if the frustration is about to enrage him to his own peril; but gradually and intelligently he begins to imitate Gilgamesh, though occasionally still throwing great straightarm haymakers that are deftly parried or ducked. The fight is by no means ridiculously one-sided, but Gilgamesh makes no attempt to land heavy punches. With growing admiration, cooled off, Engidu studies Gilgamesh's style more and more carefully, but the result is a mirror-imitation in which he leads with his right to oppose a left, etc. . . .]

[*They both laugh.*]

I grab air!

GILGAMESH

Suddenly, almost treacherously with a weird but truncated battle-cry, *Gilgamesh* knocks Engidu flat with a right hook and *bounds up the stairs out of sight.*

When you're disappointed I can see why they love you. May your tender eyes cease to show the suffering of life's love while life is still alive! —As for me, I'm already so accursed that I'd be drowned if I took notice of maledictions. So if I am day and she is night, why not fly as a white raven before I'm dead?

ENGIDU

[For half a minute he lies without movement staring up at the sky; then speaks with a new voice, though still with a slight accent. He suddenly sits up, straight from the waist, and begins to finger the IRTH on his chest. With his head high, still looking straight ahead, he rises to his knees; but then his eye wanders to Gilgamesh's axe, which he thereupon picks up to examine as he goes to sit in the lotus position at the bottom of the stairs.]

[*Silence.*]

Now I see how people are! They laughed at my ignorance when they made me think he lived in fear of wilderness. They'll cheer him when he finally lays me low. Too late I'm smitten with the city's bravest scent. Compared to him, except for her who should have been his mate, the city is seven thousand stinks. Before his nostrils flared the fight was over, and only once did the hand that felled me move; but I felt the power of something in his head not to be learned from priest or woman.

Eber enters
hurriedly.

EBER

[Preoccupied
with worry, his
surprise drops
into weary
irony.]

Oh, the little child that's come to lead us. Homesick? The fleshmonger's still got pots galore for you to dip. The duties of a human stud don't end so soon. — Ah, I see: it's guarding the tower from drunks. Is it jealous already? Or is this the way a thing-king prays?

ENGIDU

[With a wan
smile.]

Yes, oh priest-of-treasury, I am thin-king about how to tell my second birth. In the Dreamtime, invented sounds were my only words: names I sang for all things but myself: no more than that. Then Lil-Amin tutored me the pith of speech. But not enough to grasp deceit. Now I have begun to see that people can say untruth with the other meaning in each word to make the sound unmean itself.

EBER

[Kindly, taking
interest.]

Sometimes in Sumer there are meanings more than two, and no one can guess by the opposite of what is said. I can see you're not just a dumb gorilla avaricious for celebrity.

ENGIDU

[In reverie.]

I did not name the creature you say I'm not: which means I am! Before she dressed me, I was like the bandar-log, showing all my wants and itches.

EBER
[With divided attention, his eyes searching everywhere.]

Now that you know your shame, the likeness disappears. Well clothed unbelievers are more like apes than you are: not God's own creatures but golems formed by sarcastic words, civil for ambition only.

ENGIDU

You too are different. Tell me that God's name.

EBER
[With a marveling glance at Engidu.]

Are you a second Adam, that you name the beasts and seek the name of God?

ENGIDU
[Musing.]

Gilgamesh is like a god. By whatever light remains to me I'll be walking in his shadow. For him will I eat meat and drink beer, or go hungry.

EBER
[Puzzled, until he notices the broken crosier.]

What's this new note in you already? He'll kill you, unless you kill him—if you don't run away. Yes, that's it: go right now! —Oi, oi weh! You've killed the priest!

ENGIDU

No. He did. Then spared me.

EBER
[Violently distraught, he tries to raise Engidu to his feet.]

O my God, this is the end of us all! The people will riot. —Quick, which way did he go? —But first we've got to find my sons! My sons are the future, not Gilgamesh. History goes with my nation. Do you understand that this city is not the whole world? Shaddai calls upon you!

ENGIDU
[Calmly.]

I do not know your sons. Gilgamesh went up there. If Enlil rivets them both with a shaft of lightning, I'll be left to play the fool alone. To think ahead hurts more than a leg torn off. Is the debt for meat and beer this fear of what is not yet but still may come?

EBER

Tearing his hair, *Eber runs off.*

Gilgamesh is dead! I am dead! My sons are dead! —But where's the captain? Maybe he can get us out alive!

ENGIDU

My last sleep. The lion did not sleep in fear before I murdered him.

[Lies down on his side like a child and goes to sleep.]
Norkid enters briskly, fully armed. [Engidu, instantly wakened, rolls over onto his stomach, prepared to spring in any direction.]

NORKID
[Stopping short.]

Too much gallantry, Your Highness? Or were your vital fluids dried up by irony? You're doing your devotions all alone. I thought the divinities here were nothing but venereal. Some might think the people's champion has a rotten gourd; but I'd say you're sulking like a chimpanzee.

ENGIDU
[Leaping to his feet. Norkid

Why does everyone think of simians when they look at me?

NORKID
recoils, drawing his sword; but, seeing Gilgamesh's axe, he picks it up.]

Because you're a natural. Your heart is on your face. —But I've got to find my men and rip them from their screw-holes. There's trouble in the air. —What's this!!??

ENGIDU   His hawk. He did not use it on me.

NORKID   If you've killed Gilgamesh, I'll shed your
[Attacks   bones! If there's no more ground to stand
Engidu in cold   on, I'll pull the whole world down to hell!
rage. Engidu
ENGIDU   It's the ayatollah. Gilgamesh killed *him*.
catches his   Then went up those stairs.
wrist and
immobilizes his sword-arm. Engidu displays the
broken crosier and releases Norkid.]

NORKID   He's a fucking genius at outrage! What
[Laughs.]   more sacrilegious compound of desecra-
tions could even be conceived by these
bottomlanders? We'll be smothered by
the mob when this gets out. I fancy you
expect to lead the retribution.

ENGIDU   He let me live! Why did he not kill me?

NORKID   He saved you for the proper time. But
[Stares at   the people won't spare either of you
Engidu; then   when they find things gone awry. —
paces up and   Why don't you get out of here?
down   Vamoose! It's your last chance. They
thoughtfully as   pamper monkeys in Egypt. —Where the
Engidu slowly   hell are those amaranthine cocksmen of
shakes his   mine? —Shit piss and corruption,
head.]   where's even Eber and his men? —All
right then, if you want to die with us, get
off your ass and hold these stairs until I
get back with a few necessaries. The
Norkid runs off.   tower is our citadel.

ENGIDU
[Rises. Takes
up his banner-
stone.
Hesitates. Puts
the mantle
back on. Lies
down to sleep.]

Even the soldier tells me to run away. Which way is Egypt? —But no: if Gilgamesh is struck dead by her god, it's for me to inherit his statecraft. I think a black boy is capable of city-lore. For his name's sake I forswear the simplicity of escape.

Optimates hurry in, ineptly armed and out of breath. [One drags a large fish net. They are hushed in awe of the gods, and steer clear of the doors.]

OPTIMATE 1
[Optimate 2
notices the
OPTIMATE 2
broken crosier.]
Rector enters,
searching.

Engidu! The khan has broken loose! Help us catch him!

[*Screams.*] The Rector's crosier!

RECTOR

[Finds the
pieces of the
crosier.
Discovers
Gilgamesh's
axe. Engidu
sits up in
amazement.]

Enkidu! What are you doing here? I'm looking for my staff. —There it is! But broken in two! —You besotted puppet, it's a curse on you to touch it even! — Oh, now I see! Of course it was Giszax that would insult my office, and you were forced to kill him on the spot! But where's his body?

ENGIDU

[To
Optimates.]

I thought he killed you! [*Pause.*] —Now you know I'm less than he. No one can take his place.

—Do you expect to truss him up like a fish?

RECTOR
[Engidu points falsely.] *Rector runs off,* carrying the axe.

Giszax has tamed this tom cat. —Well, I'll do the job. Which way did he go? — Father Enlil, teach me a dance I was not born to learn. I'll chop down that architect!

OPTIMATE 1

This is what comes of tampering with liturgy.

OPTIMATE 2

The Rector's magic isn't strong enough. Even our godsend can't stand up against the sleepless mountain bull!

Dropping all equipment, *Optimates run off* in opposite direction.

ENGIDU
[Shifts to a position clear of the stairs and lies flat on his back, drowsily fingering the IRTH again.]

Engidu goes to sleep as *Gilgamesh slowly comes down the stairs* without seeing him, with Enlil's mask in his hand.

I could smell danger over the horizon, but when she opened up her robe, I looked. When I sat at her feet, I watched the teeth between her lips. But I did not understand. You are like a lion, she sang to me: strong and swift, a lord for women; let me take you to the house of Inanna, to the cloud-gathering peak of Uruk, where the loveless one, wise and preeminent, keeps his own counsel. Come, she said, if in your belly you crave a wife, if in your heart you long for a friend: if such desires move you. From the beginning she said such words with other meaning than she taught. But it will be bitter to sleep the longest sleep without her. . . .

GILGAMESH   Praise be to Enlil for such sweet anneal-
ment. She perfected the enclosure. I felt
her feeling me. There's a sea-change in
my bones. But still no conversion deep
enough for sleep. How was I to reach her
mind, merely on acquaintance, keeping
silence incognito? I still don't know her
thoughts, let alone her vision working at
the loom.

[He catches
sight of
Engidu,

—Engidu! I told you to go away! Why
die by the calendar?

ENGIDU   Now I know what words mean. Next
time we fight I'll have memory to help
me.

who awakens
and looks at
Gilgamesh
without
moving.]

GILGAMESH   I've just begun to cultivate the faculty
of wordlessness that you renounce.
Don't despise the instinct not to think
in action. If you remember Lil-Amin's
conduct in the dark, tell me what I
wonder: Of course she knows that as
soon as love is spent its promises renew
themselves; but would she expect a
beatific repetition before her other
senses are restored? Will the skill to
deceive be born of self-deception? . . .
When Enlil finds he's wearing horns,
I'll need your right hand to aid my war

[Laughs.]

with heaven. If she's still breathing,
which side will she be with?

ENGIDU   When she and I made jointure, it was
           you she wished to think it was, deceiving
           herself on purpose. Euoi, euoi! But she
           taught me speech sincerely, speaking of
           your fame as if you called for my friend-
           ship.

GILGAMESH Yet I am guilty of your meat and beer. If
           I live, that sin will be expiated. —Go
           back to sleep. I'd be caught asleep myself
           right now if I were more than only one-
           third human.

ENGIDU   I've had sleep enough for one who isn't
           less than two-thirds brute.

GILGAMESH Then join your share of humanity to
           mine! Let's double the manhood of this
           kingship! Multiply its liberty by two!
           The remaining necessity will be divided
           between law and nature, half-and-half.
           Let Ishtar have her sway over the things
           we do like other males; but with the guts
           of a twofold man we'll alter fate as if we
           wrote it! Pray share my follies!

[Engidu jumps   —I'll take the Rod. You take the Ring!
up and finds the
Rod and Ring, handing one to Gilgamesh,
keeping the other. They dance.]

ENGIDU   The lion will serve the eagle, and share
           his prey. I can run like the wind, and
           smell water in a sea of sand.

GILGAMESH I'll abandon my studio for the art of action, and lead the way to labyrinths; but you go first in reducing Amazons to kitties. Like wind we'll roam the world for stories, and leave this kingship to the queen!

[Engidu stops

ENGIDU But the child! Would you leave the child

dancing.] to that priest?

GILGAMESH Child? What child?

ENGIDU The child that has been started.

GILGAMESH [*Pause.*] You say I've blurted out an heir? Me, a copyist in sculpture? —Is seed entrapped by honey? Passion made me clean forget! Ishtar has us by the orchids: she makes sure the jewel of games is played for stakes. Did the gods themselves decree this rape to make me ante up. —But wait, maybe there won't be a brat! Isn't it a game of odds?

ENGIDU Not on Enlil's wedding night. I think he'll take title.

GILGAMESH By god, he can't claim my by-blow! I'll tell the world what's mine! No more his than the Rector's! My miscreant won't be circumcised and raised for stud! He was alloyed with the rarest artist. It was I, not Enlil, that melted her casting.

ENGIDU   But if he saw you, no childbirth after all: no woman will be walking down these stairs! He may have already scorned the city's oblate with his vengeance. Divine wrath, not beatitude, has been her second visitation!

GILGAMESH   Then I'll rip my tadpole from her womb, as prematurely planted, and raise him to wrest that lethal fire from the lord high god.

[Casts about for his axe without success. Takes up Engidu's bannerstone and starts for the stairs.]

—Where's my axe? . . . I'll have to use your throwing stone for surgery. —Yet perhaps it's not too late! Enlil may be slow in raising his voltage. Come on! In a god-fight I'd like to have my foster-brother watching!

ENGIDU   But now suppose the opposite. It's more likely that he's blind with rut. He'll take her second offering as the first and only. Let the eucharist run its course, without your death, or any other. —Besides, I may be the sire.

[Restrains Gilgamesh.]

GILGAMESH   [*Silence, followed by a burst of laughter.*]

I forgot that too! Everywhere we turn, your intuition outreasons mine. —You want a cub? Very well, you've jumped my claim in advance! We'll make the birthright yours. If he's born circumcised, the priest can't skin him alive.

ENGIDU   He'll look half baboon!

[Smiles.]

GILGAMESH   Your whelp will be the recognized successor. We'll stay to see him through,
and have her rear him as a bard, memo-
rizing all the feats of kingship.

ENGIDU   There can't be two of us.

GILGAMESH   We've already settled that. You're the
father.

ENGIDU   Two kings, I mean.

GILGAMESH   Why not? Our will is free. Tomorrow's
[With   combat will be a double dance of the
bannerstone in   Iso-recto-tetrahedron. Two points to
hand, he   hew each edge! We can double our talent
repeats the   for autonomy by halving the burden.
movements of   Waiting for baby, the people will have
Tablet 2.   you to love all the while I'm making
Engidu   them breed Euphrates to the Tigris!
responds in   Together, back to back, we can face both
kind, tossing   ways and never be surprised!
and whirling
the IRTH.]

ENGIDU   With me to trust, you can sleep at last!

GILGAMESH   No, sleeping's still your job. You can
sleep for two, and store it up like a lazy
lion, for us both to draw on whenever
we want to prolong our zest. Be my
dreamer too. You dreamt a world of
peace before Lil-Amin awoke you. But if
I were now to sleep, Ishtar would cackle
to high heaven that it was proof I'd been
kept awake for seven years by lack of
love.

Eber enters, in
woeful

EBER   Gilgamesh! —I find you too late already.

exhaustion,
wailing,
rending his
garments, and
tearing his hair.

—I wish it was my sons that's still alive instead of you. The apples of my eye all dead! My tribes all lost at once for good! —I'm too old to make any more baby boys for this history.

GILGAMESH
[Alarmed.]

Who killed them? How do you know they're dead?

EBER
[More calmly.]

I know nothing else. I can't find the soldiers either. I can't find anyone. This is such a hateful night that not even rumors reach my ear. —Help the Lord avenge my sons!

GILGAMESH
[Pats Eber on
the back.]

Perhaps vengeance is unnecessary, dear man. First Engidu and I will find them, dead or alive.

GILGAMESH
& ENGIDU

Questing to and fro,
We'll count the trees
And search the seas
As far as camels go!

Singing,
Gilgamesh &
Engidu go off
arm in arm,
with
bannerstone
and IRTH.

EBER

Captain! Where are the troops already? Hurry—my boys, your friends! May God lengthen your years, if you will only help!

Norkid enters
from the
opposite side,
followed at a
distance *by the*

NORKID *straggling* *Troopers,* still buckling on their equipment.	Here's the dawn patrol. They must have ended their lubricities. —Fall in, funny-boneses! Shake a leg! Strawberries and cream are too rich for your blood. Tomorrow cherries will be back in season. Dress it up, old vets! The Traders are missing. Their governor thinks they were ambushed on their way to the tents.
TROOPERS [Chuckling, giggling, and collapsing with laughter.]	—Waylaid is the word, wouldn't you say, boys? —They were still going strong when you routed us out. I've got to take my hat off to them. Nothing leaches the starch out of those merrymaking stags. —Of course they only drank a thimbleful, compared to us. But, next to those comedians, we're pikers when it comes to song and dance. Laugh? I thought I'd split a gut! —The girls did.
EBER [Shrieking.]	Girls! What girls? Where?
TROOPER 1 [Pointing the way they'd come.]	Don't worry, sir. Nothing but a little New Year's symposium. Beer, widows, and woodwinds. We had for guests some nuns.
EBER	You lie, goyim. Whoring! My sons?
NORKID	It's an unoriginal sin.
EBER *Eber runs off* to find his sons.	Oi, oi, my polluted seed! The serpent has struck at my stem!

TROOPERS
[Breaking rank,
they fall into a
staggering
shuffle and
finish up on
the ground
sprawling with
laughter.]
Gilgamesh &
Engidu return.

*We the old boonfellows of the cup and the
lance
—offered those oddfellows a memorable
chance
—to share as our moonfellows in triangular dance,
—which made us all bedfellows in
Messpot romance!*

[Gilgamesh carries the fire-stick and drill, like a
small bow and arrow; Engidu again wears the
IRTH on his chest and holds the bannerstone.
Norkid intercepts Gilgamesh at the side

NORKID
and continues
to explain the
situation sotto
voce, both
laughing.]

The lost have been found, in flagrante
delicto, and the story is an old one. The
Widows think our Traders worth their
salt.

Widows enter, beating cymbals, *with Traders*
playing recorders, in a reeling snakedance, *trailed
by Eber,* who is moaning and sprinkling his head
with handfuls of ashes from his suspended skirts.
As Rector also enters, still carrying Gilgamesh's axe,
the Troopers miraculously revive and join the
dance.
Optimates timidly reappear, fascinated, but remain
at the side.
[The Rector abstractedly and vainly thumps for
order with the butt of the axe. Then, at the horror
of seeing Gilgamesh and Engidu in amity together,
he rushes at them with axe upraised. With the bow
Gilgamesh blocks his attack and grabs away the
axe, sending him backwards across the stage, right
through the dancers, so that he ends up on his
knees, near the foot of the stairs, practically

RECTOR

*out of sight.
This violence
puts a stop to
the dance, and
all the dancers
draw back to
the right in
motionless
silence facing
the double
doors, except
for the*

Perfidious traitor! Giszax clinches his grip on the city's liver, and you fawn like a cur. Infidel! You have betrayed the people of your own creator. Salt will blight her fields; wild goats will crop her barley down to the sand. Heaven again will close. May I never speak again if I don't fix reprisal as my highest joy! Blessed shall he be who dashes the brains of your children in our marketplace!

*Troopers, who have sat down with exhaustion in
the same place, amused at their own weakness,
before realizing what goes on. The Widows thus
lean against the Traders and rest their hands on the
heads or shoulders of the Troopers. Throwing away
the bow, Gilgamesh hands Engidu the recaptured
axe and keeps the bannerstone. Together they work*

GILGAMESH

*on the doors
and succeed in
prying them
open, only to
reveal a
perfectly blank
black hole.
Each with his
weapon in one
hand, with the*

Let's spring this cage! —Gods, we've come to set you free! Are you staring wildly at each other as I say it? Gilgamesh and Engidu are coming to get the Tablets of Fate! Beware the mortal blacksmiths: Engidu and Gilgamesh are about to strike off chains. Drop the soapstones of destiny!

ENGIDU

Gilgadu on the warpath!

*other they lob the Rod and Ring into the
blackness like grenades.]
Gilgamesh and Engidu disappear into the void. After
an extended motionless silence, they reappear like
pranksters fleeing with laughter, each carrying a
Tablet, which they fling down and smash with
their axes in a fast exultant version of the IRTH
dance.*

GILGAMESH   Our dance of the twin tomahawk!

ENGIDU   I smell the feathers of an Iso-recto-tetra-
[Carried for a   hawk!
moment by the
enthusiasm of the revived Troopers (now on
their feet), the other dancers surge forward,
excited and confused.]

GILGAMESH   Ye gods that blow like the wind, you
won't forget that Gilgamesh was here.
The world is young again! Let us no
[He rips the   longer construe each other's words. —
IRTH from
Engidu's neck   My friends, it's not worthy of a pair of
and slings it   kings to dwell shrewdly domesticated in
toward the void,   this delta of marshes. —Engidu, let's go
but it goes awry   find a cedar grove with a granite quarry,
up the stairs.]   and fetch the young prince a lifetime
heap of stone and timber! An axe to cut,
an axe to hew!

ENGIDU   A blade for flesh, a blade for bone!
Engidu and Gilgamesh dance off, followed by the
Troopers, Norkid, Traders, and Eber, just as *Lil-Amin*
enters, descending the stairs in time to catch the
IRTH.
[The Urukians remaining, following the trajectory
of the IRTH, turn to face Lil-Amin on the stairs.
The Rector is exposed kneeling abjectly in her path,
whom she blesses in passing with a vague

LIL-AMIN   Vandals cannot disconcert our gods.
motion of her   Enlil is our father, and Enlil bides his
left hand.
Smiling to   time. The hour of Giszax is not yet
herself, she   come, but his felling is assured. For
hangs the   maiming the body of our motherland he
IRTH around
her neck. As
her people
watch in awed

silence, she closes and fastens the doors like a serenely abstracted housewife. All the while she is seen to be growing pregnant. She turns to the Rector.] shall be leveled to the dust, for insulting the gods of Sumer in the very house of Inanna, for suborning the consort she sent me.

—Lift up your heart: the sacrifice was full, perfect, and sufficient. Enlil finds me blameless, and the anger of heaven will not fall upon you.

RECTOR
[Huskily, in customary form.]

Save for strangers, all offences pardoned. Manifold sin and wickedness is remitted.

WIDOWS &
OPTIMATES

Amen.

LIL-AMIN   Like my mothers before me, I have been received into the blessed company of god's faithful brides, and I am absolved of mortal love by the beatitude of divine atonement. —It's still dark down here. Up on high, when I opened my eyes to the Morning Star, I saw dawn arising from far mountains.

WIDOW I   We tried to feel your holy mystery: your horrified tremors, the cold breath of Enlil, his unknown weight and shape.

LIL-AMIN   Sisters, you may well believe that my
            wedding night began in the quaking fear
            you have imagined: clammy snake, sear-
            ing dragon, clawing griffin; crucifixed
            impalement, fatal agony—anything but
            what we pray for. Yet, as Enlil's claim was
            not denied, neither was my hope. His
            pinions rocked the stars above, yet beat
            as softly as an adoring swan's, and the
            blessing was impressed that inspired in
            me a new art—not of the weaver but of
[Finding the   what is woven! Finally, in sixth or sev-
fire-bow and   enth heaven, festooned with a procession
drill, with   of beatitudes, the galaxy grew vague. . . .
solemn
playfulness she   —I could lure a man with this harp!
takes a shot in
the direction Gilgamesh has taken. When the stick
falls ludicrously short, she laughs.]

            —He found my work was good, for
            after he drew back he did not leave me
            emptied of plenitude, but returned to
            the blessing in fresh tempo. That's how
            the incubus of private love is exorcised!
            Not once along the Milky Way did the
            name of Giszax halt my breath—though
            I shall live out my life as his spinster.
[Pats her belly.]   —The child I carry is his god-daughter.
            She shall be empress of all the Sea-
            Lands. When I'm a crone at my tapestry,
            behind the altar, I'll still be teaching her
            what I have studied. Her works will put
            to shame the works of Giszax!

[To the
Rector.]

—It will take more than two king-bees to deprive this land of honeycombs. Tell the people that this year's sap and seed will flow. Children will come to birth, and there will be strength to bring them forth. Not in vain did I loosen my knees to the bridegroom and arch my throat, and press my eyelids closed, as I lifted up my spine to god. The bride you offered was not glorified in vain!

WIDOWS   *Softly run Euphrates*
Until we end this song.

Lil-Amin goes out, followed by Widows and Optimates. The Rector stands watching until they are out of sight; then leaves oppositely, ending the play.

THE ACTS OF GILGAMESH

PERSONS AND MASKS

From *The Tower of Gilgamesh*	New characters for *The Acts of Gilgamesh*
Lil-Amin and Inanna	Berosus
Widow 1	Urshanabi
Widow 2	Ziusudra
Rector (High Priest)	Mother of All
Optimate 1	Scout 1
Optimate 2	Scout 2
Gilgamesh	Shepherd 1 (Dumuzi)
Norkid	Shepherd 2 (Peleg)
Troopers	Melchizedek
Eber	Princess Enheduanna
Engidu	Villagers

FORESCENE

[Spoken by Flavius Josephus, né
Joseph ben Mattyahu he-Cohen]

Who knows how long Gilgamesh lived? There was at least one Gilgamesh on the historical list of Sumerian kings, but I mean the original hero of the epic. Was every tradition of his fate suppressed or lost? Or was his existence simply a demigod's story that had no ending? Anyway I was never satisfied with the comic conclusion of the play Herodotus wrote about him, of which here in Rome my chief collaborator discovered a copy unknown even to the author himself. Apollonius, the best amanuensis and foremost translator of my Aramaic, major domo in my Jewish Greek and Roman scriptorium, was at the time researching other things for me in Epaphroditus's library. I gave him free rein to study it because he was already interested in the attempts made by Berosus of Babylon, a priest of Baal—or Bel, or Bel-Marduk (originally Enlil)—to discover Oriental elements in our Hellenic culture. That emigrant to the island of Cos had been inspired by Mesopotamian allusions in the known works of Herodotus to write his own history of Chaldea. Without him your Elizabethans would never have heard of Pyramus and Thisbe. But even by Berosus the search for Sumerian theater was a lost cause.

With his usual gusto my Apollonius, though only a slave, dubbed himself Apollonius of Athens because he was enthralled by the epic poetry of the Alexandrian known as Apollonius of Rhodes, preferring that deracinated Panhellenist and his circumstantial details to the latterday imperialism of our august Virgil. He admired his namesake for a somewhat reactionary independence in bucking with a long narrative poem the skeptical scholars and literati who regarded that genre as outworn discursive and unsophisticated; for a practical knowledge of ships seamanship and geography; for a plain aversion to both allegorical rationalization and sheer fantasy; yet above all for the negative capability of accepting traditional myth in an age of reason, as if a new logos was wanted to generate the *muthos*! (His Muse was Euripides.) He was intrigued by the idea of Jason and his Argonauts as antecedent to the heroes in Homer.

In private familiarity I called my versatile assistant Apollo for short. I can blame him for introducing or not correcting the notorious statement in my History that Roman soldiers wore their swords on the left side. Eventually in the very first clause of my last will and testament I could do nothing less by way of benison than authorize, along with a gentlemanly endowment, his absolute manumission as a Roman citizen, in Athens or elsewhere.

Apollo was always pestering me with questions about who came before the Jews: "after all, Greeks came before Romans!". And why did the Jews (as well as the

Chaldeans before and after them) lack a theater, considering their famous love of drama and talent for acting throughout the succeeding Roman world?

His dry aspersion was a jest about my reputation for dissimulation in the old country. (His awareness of how much my reputation depended upon his willing cooperation rendered him a little too bold, but even as a slave he was by no means antisemitic.) My Roman friends called me "Son of Herodotus", having known that historiographer as "the father of lies" simply because he respected Egyptian and Persian traditions. But the frank simulations that make theater have always been under suspicion among the Gentiles, from Plato to your Augustine and his northern epigones, even unto Nietzsche who redoubled the Jewish connection. Jewish malleability, says the latter, provides "a world-historical arrangement for the production of actors." Listen to him: "What good actor today is not a Jew? The Jew as a born 'man of letters', as the true master of the European press, also exercises his power by virtue of his histrionic gifts; for the man of letters is essentially an actor. . . ." How do you like that! Were the Jews histrionic in the Second Temple (with its Corinthian columns and Greek lyres)? In the Diaspora? In the ghettoes? In hiding among Hitler's Germans? Even in the camps with chimneys?

I was indeed introduced to the Palatine by a Jewish actor after my shipwreck, but what my Roman friends chaffed me about was as nothing compared to the excoriations I suffered from my own people, especially of course the Zealots. Before High Priest and Emperor, in Galilee and Jerusalem, as general and as diplomat, on the battlefield and in the lucubrations of solitude, I have defended the factious Jews against Gentiles and barbarians—and especially against themselves! Many were the times that my life came nearly to a bloody end on their behalf. Yet it was the Romans who rewarded my profane leadership of these their most troublesome rebels.

How quarrelsome and narrowminded the Jews seemed in the days of our war! There was always an unscrupulous opposition, and opposing oppositions to both government and oppositions, orthodox and heterodox. As priests they were at best men of principle with no sense of the logical fact that high principles may conflict with each other; as fighters they ignored the political forces confronting a governor; as politicians they hardly distinguished the different functions of infantry and cavalry, to say nothing of organization, supply, or engineering. It was left to me to improvise countermeasures against the world's most effective siege army, but their thanks for my necessarily limited successes were far more than decently limited.

In Jerusalem itself I became known to the next generation as a traitorous renegade Jew—an arrogant and brutal opportunist guilty of duplicity and cowardice, serving both sides of the same war! Then as historian of the campaigns I was called boastful self-serving and tendentious, and said to be as deceitful in my writing as shifty in my actions. I was execrated by my own people as at least half pagan—at bottom a trickster and turncoat in religion too! The tactful ones called me morally ambiguous, a Janus of piety and pragmatism. Such is often the misguided infamy of a prophet who risks his life in trying to prevent a maddened beast from eating its own flesh. There were times when God really did seem to move from the Jews to the Romans. I took upon myself a high responsibility for the survival of a religious nation confused about the will of God in its rebellion against the protective power of a comparatively tolerant regime. I had warned them that resistance was folly before I reluctantly tried to make the best of their revolution. At first in command, then in thankless mediation, I served my people with devotion and grief. Along with the pride of action, the will to power, and the weight of responsibility, I felt as a private man their pain of birth, joy of life, love of family, terror of violence, doubt of intellect, loss of Temple, comfort of synagogue, and the inevitability of extinction.

Though I honored the Pantheon for its civil power and the Acropolis for its pure art, and though I revered both their languages, I was always reserved in my acceptance of Greek philosophy and Roman values. Jewish critics accused me of spiritual insensitivity, but to the very end I was teased by tolerant Romans for my unswerving loyalty to the Law and the Prophets. That didn't prevent them from erecting in Rome itself a posthumous statue of Josephus the historian.

Yet this is not the place for self-justification. I have been a public man; knowing the world, I am content with my enduring fame as a problematic but essential scholar. Without me the children of Abraham would have been mostly overlooked in secular histories. Jews, Greeks, Romans, and even Christians (whose inchoate establishment I failed to notice in my time) have used my works for almost two thousand years, at least in default of others.

Three Emperors were my benefactors and friends. In honor of my valor and skill as a former enemy, in gratitude for my diplomatic services, in admiration of my sophisticated learning, they provided me with the comfort and leisure required for mature writing (though still smiling at my personal allegiance to the lost cause of their contumacious little province). I owed them an openminded employment of the good fortune they vouchsafed me. Hence my experimental sponsorship of an Athenian bondsman's synergetic imagination.

Of course Apollo the philologist failed to discover any oriental root of Western theater for which he could claim distinct influence. The initial tributaries of almost any creation are as distant and diverse as the Mississippi's. He found no rivers Missouri Ohio or Arkansas. Perhaps a Sumerian or Akkadian drama was illiterate, or systematically suppressed. Maybe it was obviated by the arrested development of ritual, or by a precipitate decadence of liturgy that omitted its final stages entirely. An anti-theatrical prejudice probably prevailed in Mesopotamia for theological reasons. (God desires loyalty, not sacrifice, says Hosea.) But the failure of Apollo's research only kindled an enthusiasm for fabrication. This is his one and only play, intended as a complement to that of Herodotus.

With pride and trepidation he surprised me with it as a birthday present about a year before I died. You know how it is with novice poets and playwrights: they crave the praise to match their efforts. But I never could praise without perusal. Much to my eternal regret, though I made a good effort to express my gratitude and respect, I was too antipathetic toward amateur creative writers to believe that reading it would be worth preemption of precious time in my work-dominated old age. I dreaded his inexperienced challenge to the classic rules of dramatic art. I feared to find heterodoxy and sacrilege. Despite a mounting sense of guilt for hurting his feelings I kept putting him off with apologetic promises of my attention—until it was too late! Then he couldn't expect me to read it on my deathbed. Yet he declined my offer to return the manuscript neatly copied and dedicated to me in his own hand, even lovingly illuminated with symbols we had studied together. With the first tears in my eyes for half a century I asked his forgiveness, and told him sincerely that I regretted not to have adopted him as my son.

But perhaps it was not such a bad thing that not long after I was gone the original script perished with him at sea on the way home to Athens. In anachronistic comparison it is more fictitious than the *Argonautika*.

He intended it to be performed by some company of mummers that had already staged Herodotus's play about the earlier life of Gilgamesh, adding a few self-explanatory roles and dropping others, as follows.

TABLET EIGHT

[Uruk. Early nighttime in forum, by torchlight, just inside a city gate.]

Berosus sits off to one side with pestle-cymbal or darabukka drum. *Enter former Widow 2,* holding a baby to whom she is happily crooning.

WIDOW 2 *Trooper 2* *enters.*	Sweet baby mine—coo, coo, coo! Just between us, prettier than the new queen and not a day older, nor younger either.
TROOPER 2 [Kisses her and tickles baby.]	Well, the watch is set at last. What's for supper? —Me too, tiny damsel! I want some of that teat. —So are you available for fun tonight, my dearly beloved little callipyginous wife?
WIDOW 2	Cally *what?*
TROOPER 2	Beauty-ass! That's what Norkid used to call you when you were serving in the temple.

WIDOW 2 How could he know?

TROOPER 2 He wears glasses and he has a good head for figures.

WIDOW 2 Then maybe he's a pretty nice boss after all—even though he usually keeps you out all night. Shall I ask him to put in a word for you with Gilgamesh, who always seems too preoccupied to notice what a good man you are?

TROOPER 2 Don't let me catch you talking to the Captain about *anything*, that old goat! Gilgamesh has been fair enough with all of us. I pray to Mazda he makes it back here soon.When Engidu's with him he's twice too confident. Meanwhile let's you and me pluck a young mother's rosebuds while things are still quiet around here.

WIDOW 2 The way you're plucking me, our quarters will soon be too small for a soldier's happy home.

TROOPER 2 There's no place like wherever your rose bed is.

WIDOW 2 Maybe before the Rector's old glebe is all parceled out to civilians Gilgamesh will give us a little house for my bed. With a garden and two palm trees to shade another babyboo or two. I'll rig up a hammock for you to renew your virility in—if I can ever soften you up long enough for me to get some house-work done!

TROOPER 2
[Low drumbeat.]

All actors enter severally, from various directions, at first in unhurried curiosity, then with increasing excitement.

Gilgamesh will take care of us. God knows he's generous enough with our enemies, just to keep the peace. —Shit piss and corruption, another foolish night-alert! —Sorry, baby, got to go! We have the devil of a time recognizing shadows before moonrise. It's prob'ly a lion, or just some stray camel.

NORKID
[From above.]

There are at least two out there! Sound quarters!

WIDOW 2

Oh no! I'm still afraid you'll leave me!

TROOPER 2
[Hastily, as she grasps his tunic.]

For god's sake sweetheart, I'm too busy to leave you! I've got to go to the gate!

WIDOW 2

I mean it! If it isn't Gilgamesh now, he may never return! The Rector will get back his power and all you Kassites will go back to your women in the moun-tains! The kings of Ur Lagash Nippur Eridu Umma and Kish are just waiting to rape and rob us, not to mention Susa and the Hyksos raiders!

TROOPER 2   None of us will ever leave Norkid, and Norkid won't leave Uruk while Lil-Amin is queen, or her daughter. And Eber's boys are multiplying faster than your people do. That's how they count their riches, to the city's advantage. So Eber will stay when the queen asks him to, and manage everything just as he did for Gilgamesh.

WIDOW 2   But if our adventurous king *is* coming back he must have insulted the gods again. Uruk can't resist the will of heaven when its citizens are armed only with pickaxe, hod, and basket instead of bow, spear, and shield! You mercenaries alone can't man a tower and seven walls until your sons grow up, whether Gilgamesh is here or not!

TROOPER 2   Your people will learn how to fight, and
[Drumbeat   Eber's too, not just our men, if anyone
louder and   threatens the prosperity they gripe
faster. Trumpet   about that Gilgamesh has brought
signal.]   them! —Now let me go, or Norkid will put me in the guard house!

NORKID   Open the gate! It's Gilgamesh and Engidu!

Enter Gilgamesh & Engidu, ragged and dusty, one with a double-bitted axe, the other his bannerstone in hand, both with bows slung across their backs.

GILGAMESH
[To Norkid,
embracing
him.]

So it seems you've kept the city safe! How's my little daughter—and her mother?

BEROSUS
[As Norkid
replies
inaudibly.
Mingled
clamors of
welcome and
gestures of
ambivalence.
All except
Berosus
assemble
hierarchically
in the forum.]

This foreign ruler of Uruk, or Erech (as the Eberews called it), might have been Sumer's Alexander two millennia before the Greeks were ever heard of if he'd cared for power more than fame, or territory more than engineering, or religion more than his own freewill. He'd rather measure the world than win it. Though this event is long after Ea sent Oannes to instruct mankind how to serve the gods, it is many centuries before the Akkadians overran the lower valley of the two rivers.

Gilgamesh, said to be two-thirds god but one-third mortal man, tyrannical deliverer of the city, has won the loyalty of Engidu, the dark superman sent by the petitioned gods to overmatch him. With the twinned prowess of their friendship he means to double his feats. Now he and Engidu, looking ever more alike, have returned from an expedition intended to disabuse the blackhaired people of their conviction that fiery Kumbaba, hideous guardian of the sacred Cedar Forest at the top of the world (where nascent Tigris and

Euphrates are opposite trickles from the Lake of the Gods), can forever deny their brickbuilt city the timber to make it greater.

[Eber hands Gilgamesh the Rod (staff) and Ring (crown) of kingship.]

You see the pair joyfully surrounded by Norkid and his Kassites troopers. The Eberews and most of the natives are surprised to see the foolhardy adventurers still alive. Gilgamesh is greeted equivocally by the Rector and Optimates, but cordially by Eber his vizier who seats them both, and calls for cups of beer. You notice Gilgamesh from time to time peering in vain for Lil-Amin the Queen, who remains unseen.

GILGAMESH
[Addressing the Rector and Optimates.]

You said it could not be done. [*Brief chuckle:*] Prediction is fiction! A fig for your solemn prophecies! Some of you dared to murmur that I was an arrogant foreigner restless in folly, and that Uruk has no further need of lumber for its gates, rafters, furniture, and seaworthy boats. You've balked at every change in trade or speech until it's made you richer. "Enough already" even Eber sometimes said!

EBER

It's pride that I resist, not innovation. For did not Elohim say "Let not him that girds on his armor boast himself as he that puts it off." But now I'm glad to see your armor's off.

GILGAMESH   The Rector wailed that I'd bring down upon Inanna's own city the wrath of every other god because I've allowed the words of secular life as much privilege as the language of women. And I know that brave Norkid thought I was too insatiable for fame to imagine my own defeat in any matter. He believed that shape-changing Kumbaba, unceasingly alert with flaming jaws and petrifying stare, could detect the breath of a mile-off butterfly. Kumbaba's roar was said to be like the sudden thunder of floodwaters striking terror in a canyon.

Your champion, my beloved Engidu, who had lived on the steppes and come close to the mountain of the gods, confirmed these urban fears. But he was willing to share my fate. He overcame his dread and became my guide. He kept watch when I was troubled by my own childish nightmares. The time came when we had to overcome each other's fears. Yet mortal panic would have been justified. For any living creature—animal or man—the most distant view of that mountain touches an instinct of terror. Long before we mounted to its forest Kumbaba's aura froze our blood.

BEROSUS   Before they left the city Gilgamesh and Engidu had asked Lil-Amin for sympathetic advice. But according to rumor she'd only offered intimate dismay and a vivid premonition of double grief. Gilgamesh reciprocated the love in her words but ignored their wisdom. In anger at his conceited folly she withheld her blessing and refused them even an ordinary votive sacrifice, turning her back on their leave-taking.

GILGAMESH   For the city's sake, not for mine, not for Engidu's, your admirable queen execrated me with scorn for the vanity of a fastuously temerarious glory-seeking self-appointed shepherd of her people! She cursed my career of fatal sacrilege. She blamed me for corrupting Engidu— even as she tried to corrupt his loyalty to me. Neither of us laughed at the oracle. We did not deny our fear or the power of the gods. But in the end we were still refused her coldest farewell—we the sires of her daughter!

RECTOR   Blasphemy! All Uruk knows that my sister the lady-priest of Inanna did not deceive the heavenly father of our baby princess with either one of them!

Storms off, thumping his crook, followed hesitantly by Widow 1 & Optimate 1.

GILGAMESH   That woman-mongering master of ceremonies hates all reason in the name of worship. Behind my back he spits and says my feet are clay. He has no humor for the loss of his power.

BEROSUS   In those days, you see, high priests still professed their lord god Enlil to be the father in a sacred marriage. This Rector hated Gilgamesh for confiscating the temple's glebe.

NORKID   He's more unreasonable since he sacrificed his orchids.

GILGAMESH   Is Lil-Amin well? Has she been informed
[To Eber.]   that her wisdom has proved too feminine?

EBER   The queen is aware of your return. She declines to hear your story.

GILGAMESH   Before morning she'll hear it from me. You may assure her that by slighting prudence I did not belittle her warnings, or yours—or yours—or yours—or all the people's. Kumbaba certainly did terrify our entrance to the sunless Cedar Forest, and did indeed guard the Tree of the Gods. We were wearied by weeks of pathfinding, of fending for ourselves on the steppes and highlands, ever half starved or parched, always awakened from brief sleep by dreams of horror, though each of us in turn guarded by his wakeful double.

OPTIMATE 2   Tell us how you found the way, alive for months in the bush, beyond the territorial endurance of our greatest hunters.

GILGAMESH   I am no storyteller, sir! I have no time to cry or crow. Perhaps you'll find Engidu more accommodating. He's learned to speak quite well.

OPTIMATE 2   As you wish. We respect the Rod and Ring of Uruk, despite taxes and conscription.

EBER   Well you might, under an administration of justice and construction that keeps you rich.

ENGIDU

[In what follows Gilgamesh and Engidu step down at appropriate moments to act out the account in dance or mime, accompanied by the percussions of Berosus.]

When I ran with the lions I learned their fear of mountains. At first I led the way I knew, untrodden by men, between the rivers, where gazelles find water holes. Gilgamesh trusted me for forage. We ran seven times seven leagues a day, with no rest to ponder fear. But at the dark of the moon we came to drier land I did not know. I was afraid.

He took the lead. The moon came round again and made shadows with his light. Then we walked—seventy times seven leagues, more days than I could count. Gilgamesh gave me heart, found food and water when I lost hope. At night I dreamed endless fears. Finally from rising foothills we saw the cloud-gathering peak of the seven mountains still far before us at the top of the world, origin of waters. Dooming thunder shook the massif as we climbed. We dodged chains of lightning bolts from the sky at our backs.

One night on an eagle's ledge we huddled wet and cold, taking counsel. All day in hail and snow we groped for the final pass. Again we took a clinging rest to study the face of rock. At moonset, undercovered by the screech of icy wind, we pulled ourselves up to the rim of Kumbaba's domain.

BEROSUS   Thus the moon has twice made its rounds before they try their strength in that forbidden crater of the gods. Gilgamesh and Engidu each lead other in fear and feat.

NORKID   You can bend his bow that none of us can string. Now can he run as fast as you?

ENGIDU
[Suddenly exuberant.]

We have a tale that will raise the hair inside your head, if I tell it right. Before his first sight of Kumbaba, in truth, the huge heart of Gilgamesh was daunted by nothing real. As we crawled up the mountainside like tandem ants on a naked slab, with no horizon to mark a level, his longbow saved us from guardian eagles only. But when into mist we climbed the crevasse that drains the valley of the gods, blind and cautious, now and then we stopped to hold our breath and listen for Kumbaba overhead, our eyes alert for the glowing nostrils and flaming mouth that had kept intact the dismal forest of the gods since earth began by blasting intruders to dust with rays of magic, or by sweeping them deathward like dry twigs by loosing torrents from the sacred lake.

GILGAMESH   I thought it would be the fight of my life, the test and fame of mortal over fate immortal.

ENGIDU   I said: "You will not die alone. Forever we are brothers. With you together I will lose the breath of human speech and my love of life; even in this newest terror, far from all things sensible, I will fight at your side as one redoubled." But at the sound of this thought my heart came nearly to a stop, as if a god was passing. It drained the swelling of my chest, numbed my legs and arms to the ends of toes and fingers. "Yet, Gilgamesh," I cried, "there is no help in me at all! Let us turn back before the whole world is overtaken by your doom!"

GILGAMESH   But I replied: "Do not imagine weakness when our strength is multiplied by each other. You have learned the devices of man and I the skill of a lion. Do not look back at the scaled abyss; do not look up at horror." So his pounding heart grew stout again; his quaking limbs were steeled.

ENGIDU   We had taken turns climbing ahead of each other, the only way to measure our ascent into the black cloud that nullified every sense of direction.

GILGAMESH
[To the
others.]

Yes, yes, my friend, but cut it short.

—I won't succumb to the luxury of my bed until we've mustered a crew tonight and headed it for the headwaters of Euphrates. The season will soon be too dry to fetch even secular logs afloat.

—So much for your "pillar of heaven"! Look, aren't the same old stars still up there?

—The tree will be found at the foot of the mountain where it landed, scraped almost naked of limbs I hadn't lopped off with my axe before we tipped the trunk top-first over the lip. It was still more than twice as tall as the radius of its forest.

[To Eber.]

—Please recruit some good men before Engidu and I fall sleep on our feet.

[To Norkid.
Hands over a
small tablet.
He continues
to scan the
assembly while
only
impatiently
joining Engidu
to dance his
part in the
story.]

—You must make ditch-diggers and hod-carriers into lumberjacks. Give each a double-bitted axe, tempered as I've taught you. Next year they'll find easier access to the smaller timber and start some regular felling. Here's the map I made. Later I'll tell you the details.

BEROSUS
[Soft beat.]

This is not our death-day, Gilgamesh whispers to Engidu, as they come to the top of the Achaemenian Rocks, dreading that Kumbaba should hear them too soon. Engidu prays that their lives will be spared.

[Flute.]

Suddenly the silence of blackness is shattered by a shriek. The hideous face of Kumbaba emerges above them from a white fog at the very crown of the world.

[Berosus himself dons and doffs a series of Kumbaba masks.]

Even in clearing light Kumbaba's teeth gleam ghastly yellow in a red and purple gorge spitting fury.

Suddenly a fragrant canopy of green cedars is revealed above that face beneath a pure blue sky. Gilgamesh and Engidu no longer pause. Backwards step by step, holding in the breath of death, no longer panting to keep from burning up, that wily porter of the gods feigns lessening size and rage to trap the sacrilegious invaders on the bronzed alpine floor of slippery age-old needles in the deeper forest; for Gilgamesh's purpose is already known in the lamasery of invisible dieties. But as he advances, no longer daunted by reverberating screeches, he incidentally blazes the finest tree trunks for future harvest, heedless of Engidu's warning that Kumbaba laughs in mockery while leading him into impotence where retreat will be too late and any repentance will be ignored even by those in heaven who respect his fame.

Now they find themselves at the pivot of the earth where its turning shrinks to stillness. Under the noble Cedar that lords itself above all others, pointing to the pole star of the universe, they can hear their own hearts beating in the eerie silence. At poise to strike with blazing fangs, the tensed hamadryad tortures that lull with howls and hisses, swelling to fullness with gnashes of tooth and claw, shielded by leathery wings, coiling and uncoiling in sanctioned rage around the huge cedar's base like slithering roots of chthonic muscle. But the taunted champions do not hesitate in caution. Engidu suppresses fear with reckless excitement at the apparition of Gilgamesh transfigured by his renowned battle-warp, nearly as wonderful to see as the dragon's. In a unison of the mortal powers raised by action this reckless pair attacks the preternatural defender of heaven.

GILGAMESH
[To Engidu.]

[To the
others.]

Never mind the drama of it! It's not local mummery that will spread our fame beyond these walls. You can sing the feat to scribes tomorrow. Enough for now to mark the year that people from Uruk begin transhumance with an alp. Other kings and Eber's God may batten on praise for being themselves, but I want to be known for my improvement of the gods' designs. From me you have a wheel to turn your pots; bitumen that you called river dung lights the night and caulks your Sea-Land fishing boats; you trade naphtha for lapis lazuli from Kush and the people's salt from Dilmun; wood is added to the arts of stone, clay, copper, and bronze—and ciphers to your reckoning. I serve gods my own way, not by bowing down in esoteric rote. Enlil is surely not displeased that I have made seven-gated Uruk, eternal city of his daughter Inanna, proof against flood and siege. It would be too much for a soul to bear if the gods always failed to understand that canals, walls, towers, and writing too, are to their credit as creators of the people who made them—that they themselves will be magnified by the harvesting of timber for peaceful sheepfolds and temple roofs. Why should they resent my motive? Are they too orthodox to recognize my liturgies as manly worship? Anyway, I had no choice but to kill their incorrigible reptile.

ENGIDU   Gilgamesh spreads her jaws apart with the haft of his axe. I crack her skull with my bannerstone and hold her tail until he drags fifty feet of guts out by the tongue to put a stop to her unearthly death-wail!

OPTIMATE I   *Her!* You still haven't learned the pronouns!

GILGAMESH   We saw her female parts. The spawn of Tiamat. Let poets memorize what they please. Engidu is too innocent to lie for the sake of a story.

EBER
[Excited.]   The city is now returned to your hands. After the sabbath I will at last shake the dust of Chaldea from my feet. Too long with high office and rich reward you have dissuaded me. My calling is from Elohim, the One God your impiety cannot challenge. Let your servant's right hand wither if he forgets your righteousness in public justice—but excuse him now from listening to your creed!

GILGAMESH	I meant no disrespect to your nomad god, though more demanding of me than the others. Tomorrow we will reason together. You are to remain Uruk's chancellor till the moment of your caravan's departure, laden with the city's gifts.
Eber goes out, motioning for dispersal.	—Dismiss this murmuring assembly. Uruk will never be a republic.
OPTIMATE 2 [*Wallking off,* to Optimate 1.]	"Justice", forsooth! Not for Inanna's people—only for his mercenaries! I was hoping we'd seen the last of this tyrant, but now he'll be harder on us than ever. But I am surprised that lust didn't bring him and his monkey home to the queen much sooner.
OPTIMATE I [*Replying aside, as all except the following speakers go off.]*	Can't you guess why? All alone together like incestuous twins? "Guarding" each other, they call it!
BEROSUS	Thus also did the Greeks misunderstand the poem when it came down to them.
GILGAMESH [To Engidu, as *they leave together.]*	Before you take your bath go tell Lil-Amin that I'll clean up and come to bed as soon as I can. First there are other things to see to.
ENGIDU	Maybe she will still be too angry.
GILGAMESH	No doubt she's at her loom.

TABLET NINE

[Downstage right a simple cot inside a low lean-to open toward audience but initially obscured by a drop-curtain. Upstage left a small raised platform, empty at the outset.]

Berosus sitting as before. *Enter* upstage *Gilgamesh* (bloodstained), *Eber, the Rector, & Norkid.*

EBER	This is the wrath of Elohim!
RECTOR [Breathless.]	It's the wrath of Inanna! Her temple was spared. Never before have the gods shaken our land.
NORKID	Earthquakes are to be expected where I come from. So I suppose you think Mazda was always angry at us.
GILGAMESH	How much further damage? Have you inspected the walls? Any cracks in the tower glaze?
NORKID	No sign of that. Just a few leaks in some of the canal watergates.

169

EBER   Ten of the herders were killed by the cattle and about twenty of them seem to be dying. Inside the walls so many houses had collapsed that we can't yet count the dead. Most of the public wells are ruined. —But it's not the innocent gentiles that were meant to be punished!

GILGAMESH   This isn't the time to debate theodicy. Leave the dead and let the women worry about other casualties until the city is secure. Are the cattle rounded up?

NORKID   They're docile and harmless now the monster that started their stampede is dead. I must admit that such a huge aurochs was never seen where I come from. I'd like to know how he got into the stockyard before the quake! On the rampage he looked like a mammoth red-eyed lion, but he had neatsfoot hooves sharp as a gazelle's. He seemed much too canny for a wild bull that accidentally starts a domestic panic. The shaking ground may have loosened the gate but he tossed it off its hinges like an educated elephant. His horns were at least eight feet from tip to tip.

Enter Engidu downstage left, more and more slowly, attended by *Lil-Amin &* *Widow 1,* (unseen by the other players), limping across to the lean-to. He lies down on the bed.

GILGAMESH   His mane was thicker than the length of my sword. That's why it took so long for Engidu and me to kill him. It was one of those horns that nicked Engidu's foot. We are very lucky not to have fared any worse.

[To Eber.] —Send a caravan up river to get grain for the survivors' bread. We may have enough beer in your godown to tide us over till the water is cleared. Draw what

Eber leaves. you need from the treasury.

[To Rector.] —Why aren't you ministering to your people? Are you their pastor, or just a master of ceremonies? If they think that bull was sent by Enlil you can tell them that I've turned it into the greatest sacrifice ever offered in propitiation!

RECTOR Not sacrifice but sacrilege, out in the streets! Never has there been such pro-

Rector leaves. fanity!

Gilgamesh & Norkid go off the opposite way upstage, conferring.

ENGIDU [*Moaning softly.*]

WIDOW I There's no more bleeding but the smell augurs worse. He should have told you about the pain.

LIL-AMIN He imitates Gilgamesh in every bravado. He said the puncture was nothing worse than a manly scrape. But now the polluted blood has reached his head, already too late for any medicine I know. We can do nothing but apply my herbs to keep the fever down. His life will depend upon our oblations to Inanna.

WIDOW 1   Shall I go tell Gilgamesh?

LIL-AMIN   Find him if you can. See if he'll listen to a woman. Say nothing to anyone else except Norkid. If Engidu's sickness gets out too soon the Rector will call up a riot before I can assure everyone that the earthquake was not meant for us. The people are frantic enough with grief and devastation. I must attend to the sacrifice. Those who fear I'm dead in the rubble can come and see me at the altar. But I won't leave him until you bring water and my bag of herbs.

[Widow 1 hurries off.]

ENGIDU   Why are you still here? Go away! Let your ape-man die in captivity! Better alone than watched by the one who lured him to mankind.

LIL-AMIN   I am here to help you. You need silent rest.

ENGIDU   Help me! All too well I know that woman-words have deceitful meanings! You opened your robe to reveal your snare and made me learn that I was somewhat human! You cut my hair, you dressed me in clothes, you fed me meat and gave me beer to steal my strength. You tamed me for the world that thinks of death. Bitter sorrow comes too late!

BEROSUS   Engidu drifts into delirium.

ENGIDU   You were the first I saw of wordy kin! Must you also be the last? Where is Gilgamesh? It's not his fault you led me to him and death. But why doesn't he come see me die in his dungeon? You promised I would be his brother! Why does he leave me trapped like a lion in your woman-net without the strength of a hare and my thoughts too swift to remember?

LIL-AMIN   You know I did not give you this sleeping sickness. Blame Gilgamesh for folly, not me for love! He led you into evil. I gave you dearest love. I brought you to Uruk for my people's sake. They still adore you for diverting Gilgamesh from his most oppressive ambitions. You are their champion. Let them need not grieve for you. You will live if you try to remember the love and friendship among us.

ENGIDU   The promise of that love and friendship was what made me betray the gazelles and lions who ran with me on the steppes! You charmed me into hunting their kind! Then Gilgamesh made me help him taunt the gods by killing Kumbaba and the bull of heaven! —Oh save me from the dust! [*Wailing.*]

Widow 1 returns, running, with water and herbs.

WIDOW 1   My lady, please: I was intercepted by your brother the Rector and sent back to implore your immediate presence at the council. Gilgamesh refuses to consult the Optimates. They say the people cry out to be told what's happened to Engidu. Gilgamesh tells them it's more important right now to stop the looting and fix the gates. I'm so afraid of—

LIL-AMIN   Then I must go. Engidu can't bear the sight of me! Give him all the water he can swallow.

WIDOW 1   Oh my lady, I'm sorry for you—and for us all!

LIL-AMIN   Try singing him to sleep.

Lil-Amin goes off.

WIDOW 1   [*Wordless lullaby.*]

[Ministers to Engidu and draws the curtain.]

BEROSUS   Engidu sleeps and dreams.

[*Gradually diminished humming.*]

WIDOW 1   Oh Inanna, do not let our savior die!

Engidu reappears from back of lean-to, perfectly healthy, in refreshed attire, facing upstage and seen only from behind.
Gilgamesh appears stage-left in simple dress.
Inanna appears on platform (played by Lil-Amin lightly clothed as the goddess).

INANNA
[To Gilgamesh.]

I bear the blame by Father Enlil for allowing you to contaminate my god-son, and to use him against Kumbaba the warden of heaven's axis. I have defended you against the wrath of every other god. Because Uruk is my city I have also been accused of overlooking your insubordinate architecture. Yet before the council of gods I pleaded that you were a stranger ignorant of Sumerian customs. I mean to persuade my peers to withhold their righteous retribution. I will bemuse them with excuses for your effronteries and trans-gressions, promising each of them such favors as lie within the realm of love. For you are like no other man or god. Let us find a bed together. I promise your willing acclamation by the black-haired people as high king of all Sumer and the Sea-Lands.

GILGAMESH

As their beloved builder of walls and canals? As the gods' favorite acolyte? Or as your father's rival?

INANNA

Come with me to the tower's top. I will show you the sweep of your command from mountains to the sea. You shall have the means to rule all cities. Yours will be dominion over timber forests, bitumen pits, stone quarries, herds of cattle, flocks of sheep, water wells, steppes for grazing, fields for grain, and the fruit of all blossoming—everywhere between Tigris and Euphrates, and as far as you wish beyond them! You shall harvest the reeds and fishes of the Sea-Lands and build great ships to bring gold from Ophir!

GILGAMESH Everything but liberty of will!

INANNA I will forbid you nothing, not even the continued love of Lil-Amin my servant, nor of her handmaids.

GILGAMESH Is that all that freedom calls for?
[Laughs.]

INANNA What else can you imagine? Do you
[Reveals her know who I am? Do you doubt my
naked body.] promises of power?

GILGAMESH Who could doubt the power of your promise, which is not equaled by any wish in dream. I can see that you are the goddess: you cast no shadow, your eyes do not blink, your feet do not touch the ground, and there's no sweat on your brow. I further know that a deity speaks the truth of its own desire when it offers us its body. But in this case I regret that you face numinous disappointment.

INANNA Are you too haughty to sew mortal seed
[Covers herself in the queen of heaven?
totally.]

GILGAMESH   Right here in Uruk you will find such secretion otherwise available.

INANNA   It's not your child I want.

GILGAMESH   Then you ought not to be worshipped for fertility. They should praise your cunicular lust. But you envy our happiest women. Even the best of your matings with a mortal cannot convert your lovelessness to bliss. You will never know the beatitude you crave from god or man. Your body is spared women's inconveniences; so it's only compensatory justice that your freer passion should never culminate as theirs often do! As you found even with sweet Dumuzi, noblest of men, best of poets, a champion in the sport. In cruel disillusion you sent him down to dust. And all the others lured by a divinity's desire. I do not intend to end my days in thrall to your uxorious caprice or as the victim of thwarted ecstasy. Content yourself with peers who never sleep, who have never built a building or thought a new thought, whose minds are blank and clothes are always clean, whose garlands never wither, who never feel the reciprocity they miss in raping too swiftly the daughters of men.

INANNA   Revolting man! You hazard sacrilegious
conceits like a pretentious shaman! As
if you could possibly know anything
about such mysteries when you're not a
female of any species!

GILGAMESH One night nine months before I was
born in the mountains my mother was
visited by two gods imitating men.
That truth she told me later. So I know
by blood a little what it's like to be a
god. My feet touch the ground but I
don't sleep much. But I might claim to
be nearly half human in femininity! Lil-
Amin too speaks of the experience as
something opposite mine when I lose
my wits in battle-rage. You should
become more intimate with the priest-
esses that serve your temple.

INANNA   May Enlil blast your impiety! I will not
beseech an ephemeral worm! You have
seized my city, scoffed at its laws! May
you die in rubble, childless and alone,
cursed by every god for insulting my generosity, for despising my accidental notice
of your shape. You can't guess the devices
I have to rob you of the fame you crave!
If I were an earthling I'd give my life to
be your assassin. But I will find a more
painfully public drawn-out way to cut
down your towering presumption!

GILGAMESH
[Laughing
rudely.]

Does Madam Fertility Muse threaten drought famine and pandemonium for her people? —Wait! Before you go, let Engidu pay a changeling's tribute to his godmother! You can have our trophy of your mammoth Bull of Heaven!

[To Engidu.]
[Engidu throws
a knot of heavy
rope at her.]
Inanna,
Gilgamesh, & Engidu disappear.
[Berosus plays flute.]

—Flog her with the cod and pizzle! Go on, throw it in her lap! Even her father knows she's shameless!

WIDOW I

[*Croons tenderly.*]

Gilgamesh in
former dress
comes on
running.

GILGAMESH

[Widow 1
opens curtain
to show
Engidu tossing
in delirium.]

Where is Engidu? Is he really hurt? Where is he, woman! Get out of my way.

ENGIDU

[*Moaning.*]

GILGAMESH
[To Widow 1.]
[Gilgamesh
kneels beside
the bed.]

Engidu! Why didn't anyone tell me sooner? Leave those things. I'll watch tonight.

ENGIDU
[Suddenly sits up in agitation.]

No! Don't come near me! Now I know your heart! Always false brotherhood with nice words! . . . When you said I was your friend Eber smiled like a father and called me Nimrod the mighty hunter. Norkid made me welcome to the soldiers. . . . You kept me so much at your side that because of our likeness people called me the Good Gilgamesh. Passing in the street they began to say "We are not blind. That's the real Gilgamesh, disguised by Inanna as barbaric Engidu!" . . .

BEROSUS
Widow 1 goes out.

So began in Engidu's delirium the legend's amalgamation of two figures. This hierodule watched and listened but she was an imaginative witness. Afterwards she told migrant traders disparate stories about the same personage.

GILGAMESH

My dearest friend, I was pleased with the confusion. We have not ended our feats, for yet more fame in greater deeds than killing. You must get well soon, so that together we can astonish the gods with acts of peace.

ENGIDU
[Not listening.]

. . . Your smiles grew false with jealousy of the people's love. Yet still you used me! Without me you could do nothing great enough to keep Uruk in docile subjugation. . . . You were clever; I was just an uncouth brute, easy to deceive. . . .

GILGAMESH   Engidu, are you saying what you really mean? How did I deceive you? How could I? Why on earth should I of all men have need to play you false as twin to my own heart? I wanted the people to love you! I saved your life and you saved mine! You were afraid when I was not; I was afraid when you were not! We loved the same woman! If you had cared about kingship I would have gladly shared the Rod and Ring!

ENGIDU
[Gilgamesh raises his head to give him water but then meets agitated resistance as he gently presses him down again.]

You have turned me against lions and aurochs, and even against the gods. Yet you never let me be my own man! What have I become but a savage in captivity, dying alone in this cage within the walls of a city I hate! . . . You lured me with words that never meant what people told me they said.

GILGAMESH
[Lays his head against Engidu's chest.]
Lil-Amin enters quickly but pauses to watch from a short distance. When Engidu notices her she comes to stand beside Gilgamesh.

You wrong me, Engidu—after all our time as loving equals! I who understand more than other men cannot guess what mistaken thought has turned you against me!

LIL-AMIN   The gods have taken his reason. We can only pray for him to sleep.

GILGAMESH   You pray. I cannot pray. Where is your magic now? The gods rule by doing nothing. The people prayed for him but their love cannot keep him alive! They are always answered by what they're told's the will of heaven.

[Impulsively he rises and rips from her neck the Isorectotetrahedron, slinging it by the lanyard into the audience.]

—This jewel I gave you is only my mnemonic symbol, not an amulet! A real rectotetrahedron changes shape in reason's nightmare! Life's edges and facets are never so neatly fixed. Our world is not a constellation in the sky! It slips away from us like an altering dream, less to be trusted than a river of moons. Let Euphrates drown every gem like this!

LIL-AMIN   You can't throttle grief by recanting your own reason! If you can't pray to gods, proud Gilgamesh, pray to yourself. Even you may be capable of that! Pray to realize the fact that Engidu is dead.

ENGIDU   I go! You stay.

[Engidu dies.]

GILGAMESH   His eyes are clay. Inanna has killed him!

LIL-AMIN   Your tears become you now, the only offering to gods I've ever seen you make.

TABLET
TEN

[The queen's reception chamber. Two formal chairs side by side upstage somewhat right of center. One is occupied by *Lil-Amin,* motionless and apparently listless in mourning; the other is empty. *Norkid* stands or paces upstage like a self-effacing bodyguard. *Gilgamesh*, unkempt, his back turned to the chairs, as if in an inner room downstage left, is working awkwardly on an inchoate stone statue, little more shapely than a stele, of about his own height mounted on a sculptor's swivelled stand. A few apparently cuneiform characters are lightly visible on its base. Engidu's bannerstone serves clumsily as both mallet and chisel. His own double-bitted axe lies nearby. *Berosus* sits as narrator and musician in his usual place on the right side.]

[Without interrupting his work Gilgamesh beckons to Norkid, who advances stiffly toward him.]

GILGAMESH   Has Eber at last left me?

NORKID   With his people and his chattels.

183

GILGAMESH   I thought he might postpone his departure until the obsequies were over. More than ever I need him now. That is to say the city does.

NORKID   Yes sir.

GILGAMESH   You saw him off?

NORKID   He was my friend.

GILGAMESH   He at least didn't die.

NORKID   We are vulnerable without those Traders and their caravans.

GILGAMESH   But especially without his management. Had he no compunction about leaving us at exactly our weakest moment? Even gravediggers are distraught by women keening with lacerated lips and clawing at their own eyes to enlarge the flow of tears. I wish I were able to console myself by howling with them. Did Eber express no regret at giving up his power here?

NORKID   He'll remember that loss when he's at last shaken all our dust from his feet and his fear abates.

GILGAMESH   It's absurd to fear another earthquake here, any more than he might have feared one before now. All along he's needlessly feared the wrath of his God for serving me. Is there something new in his usual displeasure with my lack of policy? There has been no ominous death in his family. Perhaps I've stayed too long in seclusion. Did he leave any explanation or apology?

NORKID
[Gilgamesh stops work without looking at Norkid.]

He only kept repeating "Pride goes before a fall, and a haughty spirit before destruction." Referring to what he calls your murder of Engidu.

Rector enters ceremoniously carrying an abstract iconic figure representing the god Enlil, which he places in the seat of the empty chair. He is accompanied by Optimates & Widows. Norkid turns back to stand behind Lil-Amin. Flute music by Berosus.]

GILGAMESH
[Looks over his shoulder; slowly drops his tools and moves to center stage. He speaks wearily.]

Is this new ceremony of yours meant to remind me that Engidu once sat there? Or is it an attempt to usurp the kingship by reclaiming the rod and ring for yourself? If you weren't the queen's brother you would have been removed even from your present office for clandestine resistance to my assumption of sovereignty. As magus and pontifex maximus you must stop meddling in affairs of state. Don't dare take advantage of my mourning.

RECTOR
[Boldly.]

You have killed Engidu, sent by the gods to relieve us of your tyranny! The Lord God Enlil is our only king.

GILGAMESH   I saved your city from the Elamites,
built its walls above the highest floods,
and bonded it to gods with an imperishable tower as a ladder down from
heaven. I have made Uruk preeminent
in prosperity and power under a rule of
reason and justice. Yet you continue to
instigate the seething disparagement of
me as a godless rebel against heaven, a
savage northman civilized only by the
people he subjugates. I am weary of
engineering the excellence of a city that
denies me credit. With Engidu's death I
have outlived the satisfaction of public
works and the pleasure of invention. I
am ready to renounce the hope of constructive adventures. But who will
make a better shepherd for this people?
I vow that you will not succeed me!

RECTOR   And now you have prevented Engidu
from doing so. Whoever is chosen by
the queen must be a king that banishes
strangers with foreign words and what
they mean; one who will not destroy or
scorn our rites. I speak for the temple,
I speak for the people, I speak for the
queen herself!

LIL-AMIN   I speak for myself, brother.
[Apathetically.]

She and Norkid remain impassive as *Rector,
Optimates, & Widows walk off* ceremoniously.

GILGAMESH	Norkid, for whom do you speak?
NORKID	I am loyal to the queen.
GILGAMESH	And no longer to me?
NORKID	The death of Engidu absolves me, except as she may direct me.
GILGAMESH	You really believe I killed him?
NORKID	You caused him to die in the prime of innocent strength. Even as your old dog I howl with the people at such unnatural death.
GILGAMESH	Wisest of soldiers, old Kassite friend, how can you be so blind? Are you so affected by their religion?
NORKID	Too much invention is intolerable to anybody's gods. Your kingship was too defiant.
GILGAMESH [Ironic tone.]	*Was!* Do you and the Council consider me deposed? With the troopers in my pay? No doubt incited by the effeminate priest and ratified by his puppets. It's strange that no one has dared a word of mutiny until I now pry it from my oldest friend! Of course I can remain the shah if I pretend not to notice the honest tense of his speech. Or are you simply anticipating my assassination? —But if retribution comes from gods, why haven't they long since killed me?

NORKID   Perhaps they waited to strike with a blow that's harder to bear.

GILGAMESH   Then they are perceptive after all. The
[Turning back   nothingness that follows life of course
and forth.]   knows nothing of its loss. But for me the loss of another's uniquely beating heart, which you say I myself have caused, forever feels the extinction of a life as precious as my own. My tardy wisdom comes with grief and dirge. My lifeless works have gone for naught as far as I'm concerned.

—But for the gods' sake, as well as the people's, it would be stupid to neglect canals and walls now that they exist. They serve both species. Teach the people you've joined to consider them monuments to Engidu, the creature sent by heaven to destroy my pride. That's all I still ask of you.

—Without you and your Kassites at my side this city would still be little more than a disputed place for fording the river. Together you and I liberated from Elamite vandals the ruins these new wonders of the world are built upon. Without you, for that matter, I'd still have been wandering the world for something to do like an impoverished knight. And without you, as staunch older brother, I never would have mated with this queen and found my twin! For me the sorrow broadened by the threat of your defection would belittle the loss of all that we have constructed. You now deprive me of whatever solace I might have found in mourning.

—But no more foolish speculation about eliminating me! With or without you, I remain king, much the wiser.

Norkid runs off, doubled over, covering his face. [Gilgamesh removes the idol of Enlil, setting it behind the chairs, and sits in its place beside Lil-Amin.]

LIL-AMIN   Have pity on that good man's unhappiness. His thoughts hurt him more than the wounds of torture. He will never betray either of us.

GILGAMESH   Does displeasure with me drown your lamentations? And is denunciation easier for you than it is for Norkid?

LIL-AMIN   My allegiance is to Enlil and Inanna. I wish I had told you before their patience ended that I could no longer allow you in that place by me.

[Indicates the chair. He jumps up and steps aside.]

I don't need anybody's chair or bed!

GILGAMESH   —Then it's true that even you blame Engidu's death on my impiety?

LIL-AMIN   I shall not darken the enlightenment of
                your rule or defame your arts, but I was
                wrong to let you loosen my religion in
                gratitude for your liberation of this city
                and in bemusement with the distinc-
                tion of your manhood. But you were
                not willing to defy the Tablets of Fate
                without enlisting guileless Engidu to
                share your guilt. As your mirror, an
                actor of your will, he was damned.

GILGAMESH   It's true that I gave not much thought
                to his soul. But—

LIL-AMIN   Nor to anyone else's!

GILGAMESH   I spared you implication in most of my
                transgressions.

LIL-AMIN   Because to you the royal priestess of
[Suddenly   Inanna was but a captive yoni, otherwise
animated.]   distinguished as nothing more than a
                weaver of indoor pictures. I was for spo-
                radic recreation from your daily operation
                of a public labor machine, or for carrying
                whoever's child might win the game!

GILGAMESH   The art of weaving is higher than any of
                mine. And in your absurd indictment
                you don't mention that our recreation
                has always been in a bed of love.

LIL-AMIN   I've learned from you a manly silence.
                At first I thought of you as the mildest
                of kings, gentlest to women, boyishly
                besotted by the lure of glory. Now I'm

not content with occasional addresses of the consort thigh and solemn advice on how to manage the state in its absence. I can't believe I ever thought of love! For a woman of my kind it brings the unhappiness that exceeds all others. The people deserve a competent queen—to honor their cult and conduct herself as a regal mother. My daughter needs the love that surpasses the love of unhappiness.

—Yet maybe she will inherit and esteem much of what I did love you for.

BEROSUS
[Aside.]

My history reports that the princess later did so, married elsewhere to imperial power, a harder woman than her mother.

GILGAMESH
[Returns to his work downstage.]

I hardly recognize you as the person I have loved. Is it motherhood that's made you inimical to me? Or was your soul cured by the shaman's behest to "know yourself"— pernicious counsel to anatomize your heart and cloud your reason. Don't you even remember your past feelings? Do you really deny our matchless affinity?

LIL-AMIN

Yes, matchless by any two others but not a match for us! I repudiate my illusion without forgetting it. You are replaced by my proper responsibilities.

GILGAMESH   Engidu was witness to my loyalty when I spurned your goddess. She promised me chariots of gold and lapis lazuli, and gave assurance that my goats would multiply in triplicate! I might have thought that in your heart you would recognize my fidelity to love and value in refusing the carnal Muse herself.

LIL-AMIN   I am the servant of Inanna, not her rival.

GILGAMESH   Yet your disaffection is colder than I thought possible for the chief priestess of her temple. No wonder your people and my own soldiers have joined your brother and his puppets in execrating my alliance with Engidu.

LIL-AMIN   Not the alliance but your fatal abuse of it! You still fail to understand the city's solidarity of hope—and how you doomed it.

GILGAMESH   Yes, I fail to understand why I'm blamed for the first death I've ever felt—I who part even with you, and dismiss a whole life's famous accomplishments, to contemplate Engidu's extinction! I for whom he was loving and beloved brother! I whose life was many a time hazarded with his and thereby doubled! Am I so untutored in sympathy that I cannot understand the public's mourning for a champion hardly to be distinguished from myself at our usual distance from the common eye? I did not seek to learn compassion by the pain of a loss wholly beyond the imagination of keening women.

—What can causes matter after death?

LIL-AMIN   You are cruel to include me in the public. Or Captain Norkid, without whose excellence you'd still be a vagrant privateer.

GILGAMESH   Never mind *Norkid* and me! You're the one who cannot understand the many-knotted bond of service and command. Speak only of Engidu and me.

—I do not think of you in any class of beings, but you have joined the commons in holding me at fault for the first despair in my life. Until the final adventure with my peer, most of my thoughts were hopeful and active, never disappointed. I was as innocent of compassion as a lion. My foresight was for worthy public things, my heart a bobbing cork of innovation, unanchored to the bottom of life. Then came Engidu to complement the private unity I thought I had with you. With him I could undertake benign expeditions and glorious feats too difficult for a single champion. But the extinction of culminating hopes has awakened my heart to the vanity of those I'd realized. I'm a plummeted bust of stone staring

[Indicates the stele.]

groundward from the floor of the sea, with no more ambition than this lifeless matter, which I can hardly see in a sea of tears when I look at what I'm doing!

LIL-AMIN
[Softly.]

It would be a truer image of Engidu if you let me make it of clay on my potter's wheel. Fired it in your kiln, it would endure as long as stone.

GILGAMESH

No clay, never never clay! I saw his eyes fade to clay. He no longer heard my voice. His face was white, his lips were pale, his chest was hard. I thought we'd always be together, but I saw him petrify in revulsion from life's oven. Yet not too cold to incubate the worms that before my very eyes began to crawl from his ear, then from his nose and mouth! If mad I am, that's the horror that drove me mad. So I limn his effigy now in colorless rock, the precious last piece of Elamite stone stockpiled for my towering vainglory. Worms cannot live in faces made of granite.

LIL-AMIN

There would have been no worms if you hadn't kept his body from the tomb so long. Ungodly mourning has disturbed the people more than godless deeds of the past. It was madness to prolong your weird dirge—without considering public, priest, or queen—in your transport of newfound pity for a living creature because he might have

been yourself! As always, too enrap-
tured with your own excesses to heed
any nation's law or custom!

GILGAMESH
[Loosing his
anger.]

How can the lady soul-doctor open her
mouth with such infuriating exaggera-
tions? I won't listen to such asinine
clairvoyance about me!

—Only fire could have killed those
loathsome maggots! But Norkid threat-
ened tripartisan sedition if I tried to
cremate Engidu's corruption! Even the
best-educated Kassite really believes that
sacred fire must not be polluted by a
dead body! I have no covenant with gods
but in affiliation I do address the all-
burning sun. Utu does not scruple to
burn parched fields and their vermin!
But your people abetted Norkid's opposition by clamoring for the wormy ditch.
Even before Engidu was dead the Optimates ordered his grave, and citizens
were sent out to glean bricks and shards,
as if to hide a midden!

LIL-AMIN

The tomb was properly ready long
before you let go of the corpse. I promised that the chamber would not be
closed until you laid your imperishable
effigy by the body's side, but for fear of
plague the sepulture's sealing can be
postponed no longer.

GILGAMESH
[Turns back to his work with renewed energy.]

I'll soon be finished! Neither worms nor fire will disintegrate this apparition of the mighty hunter they call Nimrod, Gilgamesh's only partner.

LIL-AMIN

The commonwealth cannot continue to indulge your nobly morbid lamentations, which I think express more than anguish for your best friend.

GILGAMESH

Now don't tell me to know myself! May Utu curse all feminine divinations!

LIL-AMIN

In any case there's no more time for pity. We well know that misery comes at last to the healthiest of men. Deer and lions weep; wild asses too; priests, widows, farmers, and servants weep. Our river weeps, the other river echoes. It is said that "Every man must give up the days that are lent him, and take up his dwelling elsewhere." Engidu's house is large enough to add Semiramis and me: but stuff it with what you wish!

GILGAMESH

I curse your superstitious custom! Engidu's pyre would have been atop my tower, filling the night sky with solar glory. That beacon would have been remembered unto the last generation by all the wild creatures of the steppes and by the gods who love high sacrifice but do not notice the puny mounds that keep mankind's memory alive between dust storms. But at least this stone, half formed by an insane artificer, will never die!

LIL-AMIN   Since you can't infuse the breath of life.

GILGAMESH   When I was young, thinking forward and outward only, seldom lingering in reflective meditation, naturally the death of self, or of my mother, did on occasion cross my mind; but it would instantly dissipate into the stream of my appetites and plans—even as I saw more of violent death than most men did, and certainly reckoned on it for many who opposed me. I'd been told, and never thought of questioning, that I was two-thirds god. So I was never curious about how it feels to die.

—I suppose you believe that even in my present hopelessness I'm still too armored with congenital hope to contemplate an end to the one who hopes—that I have too long claimed the fame of defying necessity. In part you are right. But the shock of Engidu's death and an unfamiliar numinous fear has awakened me from the sleep of reason. Never more shall I ignore the mystery I share with every animal and human. Yet not for me is soul without a living body! —All my designing here is done. You must finish what's begun.

LIL-AMIN   Gods themselves weep for the death of mortals who serve them, some of whom are children of their own. But you think it's the fear of death I see in you, when I know your thinking has a nobler cast.

GILGAMESH   How can I trace the path of time?

Dropping his tools, *Gilgamesh* lifts the heavy statue to his shoulder, takes up his axe, and *carries them off stage,* accompanied by Berosus's darabukka drum.

LIL-AMIN

Lil-Amin picks up Engidu's bannerstone. Calls after Gilgamesh. Then stops to pray before *following him off.*

Here, take Engidu's own axe for the grave! Lady Inanna, spare the people. The fault is mine alone for weakening to the sacrilege of an overlord. And keep safe my daughter, your father's child, to live out her destiny in a city that honors the laws handed down from heaven.

TABLET ELEVEN

[Upper edge of an island's flat beach. *Urshanabi* squats looking down at *Gilgamesh*, who is prone on the beach before him, axe in hand. (He wears not much more than the small Iso-recto-tetrahedron slung from his neck on a thong.) On the sand in a transverse row between them are seven loaves of bread. Nearby lies a gourd of water. *Berosus* as usual sits off to one side.]

[Gilgamesh raises his head to look at the loaves.]

URSHANABI   Can you stay awake now?

GILGAMESH   It was miraculous to recover breath enough for sleeping! I dreamt there were seven giant stone men above my brow to keep me from getting off the beach!

URSHANABI   Eat the bread. There's sweet water. I thought you were a dead man.

GILGAMESH   So did I.

URSHANABI   How did you get ashore with that axe? Even when you were sleeping I couldn't get it out of your hand. It's something that may be useful on this island.

GILGAMESH   I swam with one hand. That axe is all I have. No use landing without it.

URSHANABI   Well now the Mother of All Living has proved The Ancient of Days wrong. He said you must be some demigod, since Enlil has drowned all mankind for being too troublesome and noisy. But gods don't sleep. She baked a loaf every day you lay there to show how long you slept. She expected you to want the truth.

GILGAMESH   I'll never sleep when I reach the sunrise. I fell asleep while she was talking, but I thought it was in the dream. An old man and an old woman were droning over my head.

URSHANABI   The surf was up. They came to watch and noticed you tossed by the breaker. There's not much of a tide here, but it left you high enough to be hauled the rest of the way up the beach when they called me to help. You were very lucky to be washed through the western passage in the reef.

GILGAMESH   My boat had been once too often patched. In fact I didn't think it would last that long. The reeds were waterlogged and finally the pitch gave way. I was paddling with the axe head. That at least was no dream. And I don't think I've dreamt you up.

URSHANABI   I'm just a carpenter who's lost his tools.

GILGAMESH   I'd prefer to address you by name.

URSHANABI   Urshanabi, but Ziusudra still calls me Sailor sometimes.

GILGAMESH   Who is this worthy Ziusudra?
[Still dazed.]

URSHANABI   Was. King of Shuruppak, he claims; also originator of sacrifice and auspicy. The wisest and most virtuous of soothsayers, his wife says: therefore entitled to the honorific Atrahasis. He told me he was warned of a flood by the voice of a god. But it was I and my raft that saved him and his woman. We found that our river had no mouth: we were swept out to sea before I could pick up something to steer with. What we haven't salvaged for the fire is rotted driftwood now. —Well then, who are you?

GILGAMESH   I hardly know. Give me time to think
[Gets to his feet   my way back out of dreams. I must
and stretches. Peers   thank the lady for my daily bread and
at the bread.]   pay my respects to the governor. I think I remember seeing their faces.

URSHANABI   There's no one here to be governed but me.

GILGAMESH
[Points to the sky.]

So I surmised. —Which way is sunrise? Is the sky always so overcast?

URSHANABI

Aside from typhoons, very seldom. I suppose it's a sign you've brought us bad luck. But I would have been glad to see any human being, though a young woman would have been more welcome.

GILGAMESH
[Drinks water and starts eating bread.]

I am no enemy. But where are Ziusudra and his lady now?

URSHANABI
[Points landward.]

The Ancient of Days and the Mother of All Living are off in the bush for their daily attempt to breed a new race. Since your avatar they've shunned this beach as wanting in privacy. He told Ziusudra to sire four sons, each to start his own new tribe. I am to be midwife. So those two survivors have been going at it three times a day ever since the Lord God Enlil amended his curse on the teeming world. All the other gods had raised a clamor for the restoration of public services and earthy women's favors.

GILGAMESH

In his ire Enlil sometimes forgets that without human work there would be no canals to water fields of grain, and no altars for the sacrifice of flesh.

There'd be no leisure in heaven. Gods would be laborers, or go naked and hungry. —What will Ziusudra do for daughters-in-law to bear fecund grandchildren?

URSHANABI   It is said that Inanna will produce them from this island's clay, all in good time. But the question is moot because Mother of All doesn't tell the Wise One that she's too old for babies. I suppose she likes his efforts. Meanwhile she spares him the burden of any other work if I can't do it. She is convinced that an archiflamen who studies gods' messages in the night sky can't be expected to pick coconuts, gather seaweed, or go fishing.

GILGAMESH   The gods chose a friend of mine for death, and it didn't require a flood. What about livestock and all the other creatures living on each other to feed or clothe those who served the gods? Such a flood must also have rid the earth of snakes and cats. Ospreys and their like might survive on fish, but the other birds must have perished.

URSHANABI   Ziusudra made pictures of all the birds and beasts, male and female, to preserve the species. He grieves more for the animal kingdom than for his comforts and servants.

GILGAMESH   If I had thought life could be preserved
               by pictures I'd not have taken the trou-
               ble to fix words with writing. How did
               he save so many tablets on a raft, or
               even cylinder seals?

URSHANABI   For one who counts the stars and com-
               municates with gods it is not difficult: he
               stored the pictures in his head. He's
               learned everything that I don't under-
               stand.

GILGAMESH   You can see in the stars what takes your
               fancy. I have seen a raging bull.

URSHANABI   It's not his wisdom that makes me glad to
               serve him. Nor the riches that will be my
               reward if his expectations come to pass.

GILGAMESH   I'll ask his advice, and yours. But if this
[Finishes   ocean is an ephemeral inundation,
eating bread.] when will it subside?

URSHANABI   He watches the irregular reach of waves
               on the sand for hours at a time, and
               chases the retreating surf to reclaim the
               margin of its undertow. And as the tide
               ebbs he follows it patiently with hope.
               When he can no longer deny its return
               he says it's still just practicing for the
               ultimate revelation of basic earth. He
               declares that it tastes less bitter every
               day, and that when it's sweet enough to
               drink our shoreline will begin enlarge-
               ment. We shall find ourselves on a
               mountain peak.

GILGAMESH   That reasoning is not unsound. He sounds like a patient prophet.

URSHANABI   Here they come. Maybe he'll have the pleasure of finding out who you are! He may even answer some of your questions. —I must get ready for cooking.

Enter Ziusudra
& Mother of All
Living.
[Urshanabi
hastily busies
himself.]

ZIUSUDRA   Speak, apparition! You look alive at last.

GILGAMESH   Thanks to your kind lady and this affable sailor.

ZIUSUDRA   It looked as if the flood had drowned you, but we couldn't let a survivor starve. How did you escape the common fate? I wonder if you are one of my descendants. If so, you must have heard of me: Ziusudra, sometimes Utnapishtim in legend: secretary astronomical, master of ceremonies, royal Atrahasis in any case, so entitled by the gods. Why do you disturb the proper succession of things?

GILGAMESH   I journey east on Utu's road. But always sunrise seems as far ahead as ever.

ZIUSUDRA   The sun rises over there and beyond. From the other side of this island you can look toward the world's east edge, but it's still too far to see.

[Points
inland.]

BEROSUS   I don't know distances by sea, and I'm not a scholar of time.
[Aside.]

MOTHER OF ALL
[To her husband.]

No one can get there. —Even to find his father a stranded son would be suicidal to waste his salvation by ignoring the facts.

GILGAMESH

Madam, your words betray some clairvoyance—but no mortal has ever wished more than I to stay alive. In youth I paid no heed to time until I found that my friend Engidu had not had his share of it. He was seized by the earth like some creature of a day. Now he's curled in that black womb, disintegrating in slime that turns to dust, uncohering from unique personality into a million common atoms less alive than the seed of fossils. Now I always face the morning sun and put the afternoon behind me, striving to see time's arrow at the bow.

ZIUSUDRA

You may as well search for the winds. Time is the gods' mystery. Can you be so privileged? If not, you will go blind seeking such light. You are speaking to a seer.

GILGAMESH

I have no wish for second sight. The very simplest knowledge of here and now is what I want. Let come what may. Prophecy is fiction. I leave that to you. Time was before the Tablets of Fate. Even your gods themselves can't overcome what doesn't come by necessity unless it's already here.

ZIUSUDRA   May I ask by what name such a polem-
ical monotheist distinguishes himself
from slender-witted madmen?

GILGAMESH   Call me Noman. I hope for advice that
only you as a scholar of the skies can
give. As long as I'm learning I'll teach in
return.

ZIUSUDRA   I'm intrigued by the offer if you're as
clever as you sound. But Mardi is my
kingdom now. This is the end of the
rainbow. You must do my bidding.

GILGAMESH   As long as you are just. I wasn't born to
be subjected.

ZIUSUDRA   This is an island of no return.

GILGAMESH   There is nothing I wish to return to.

ZIUSUDRA   Where do you come from? Who really
was your father? How did you escape
the flood?

MOTHER OF ALL   No no, my dear. Let Noman tell us as
he wishes, a little now, a little later.
Everyone's story reveals its causes, and
when pieced together anyone's story is
worth waiting for. That way he'll tell us
much more than what you can think of
asking. You won't have to speculate so
much. A friendly way is always best. Let
him take his time. He's suffered much
in getting here. Any tale is better than
none.

ZIUSUDRA   All right. I am tired of my own news.
[All except
Gilgamesh sit
down opposite
Berosus to
listen.]

GILGAMESH   I may have strayed off course. This is
the same earth I've always lived on but
the stars here are new, or too low to recognize. —How much do I remember?
Certainly not my two fathers. I'm not
even sure how many of my memories
may be dreams.

MOTHER OF ALL   Please don't worry about needless dis-
tinctions. Sometimes we too confuse
one kind of memory with another, and
some are false perforce. Just as you and
I forget some of the truth that we used
to remember.

GILGAMESH   For me there's often too much to
[He   remember. At times in stress I forgot to
accompanies   stay on a straight course to the sunrise
much of his
narrative with by keeping the pole star on my left
dance or   without crossing the ecliptic to my
pantomime,   right. But there was no way to observe
moving from   both those marks at any one point
point to point,
with his axe, in unless I stopped for a night and a day.
illustration of But when I sojourned for a while,
his travels.]   repossessed by habitual interests and
pleasures, I was likely to forget the purpose that drove me.
—Yet I do remember the greatest challenge to what was still my youthfresh
strength. Two lions tried to deny me

water and a share of their kill at an isolated spring. They may have been
former companions of Engidu who
held against me his decadence and
wormy death. Of necessity I killed
them both, each with one blade of this
axe. —Then trekking an immense plain
eastward, I was daunted by the barrier
of an endless mountain range gradually
rising in the east. The massif of unscal-
able cliffs was surmounted exactly in
the center of my direction by two
broad-based peaks like upright fangs of
heaven guarding the nativity of time.

BEROSUS
[Aside.]

Thus his memory.

GILGAMESH

That night two giant scorpion-men
stood guard over the pass between the
peaks. They seemed to see both ends of
time. I hailed them. They conferred
together, bending across the alpine
space that separated them. I held up the
axe to show my only weapon, calling up
to them my name and purpose. Again
they whispered through the void of
stars. Then they turned again and
pointed down into the recess that separated them, one with his left hand and
the other with his right. Accordingly I
advanced and beheld that I had been
deceived in perspective. The scorpions
had been standing on two separate
mountains overlapping like crooked

teeth, split apart by a bending canyon no wider than my shoulders. For seven nights and seven days I groped and wended through that deep fissure, dark as a cave, ever fearful of wedging myself into a jointure of sheer walls as parallel as a frost-crack's, where my skeleton would stand upright till the end of the world. But at last, as I was about to succumb to thirst, I was revived by an errant ray of the risen sun briefly penetrating the twisted darkness ahead. I forced enough hope from a kindred spark of life to claw myself many hours later out upon the gentle eastern slope of that sierra, next to a purling brook, just as the day was ending.

BEROSUS
[Aside.]

Thus his dream.

GILGAMESH

When I awoke the sun was rising as far away as I'd ever seen it. But my feet were cold and a beautiful girl was rubbing them. For many days she kept my attention. I recovered my strength. She had been lonely. She had been yearning for someone worthy of her first love, and she was well prepared by imagination to make me forget for a time everything that she had no interest in. She diverted me with reciprocal usages she wished to learn. For a long time I gave myself up to the pleasures of tawny skin like the lion of a pride. I lingered in her pleasure garden with amber beer, among the peaceful people of that broad valley.

BEROSUS
[Aside.]

Memory of the Harappa flood plain.

GILGAMESH

Day and night, nothing—no one in the circle dance—was denied me. A black panther was my bodyguard, purring at the foot of my generous bed. No strife, no jealousy, among that moonlit people! I had bells for my toes and elephants to ride on—but a ring on my nose! So when I paused from idle recreations my mind began to recall old motives. They allowed me to make plans and build a city safely on the river bank, with watered fields and gated canals to carry their freight. I also taught them how to write and reckon.

The ring had fallen from my nose, but still for too long I was distracted by constructive pleasures—as if I was seizing the chance to build a greater Uruk with an exotic labyrinthine tower! It took seven years and more for me to learn that public improvements are always in progress and decay, never finished. . . .

MOTHER OF ALL

Sir, you lose us in your memories!

GILGAMESH   Anyway I noticed that I had forgotten both the bitterness of private loss and my essential quest. I had forgotten myself in the bemusements of dalliance and engineering! To my horror I woke to the understanding that I was still captive to a gratitude greater than any I had known before, and to a young woman's instinct for godlike babies, threatening to lift her skirt to the wind as my mother did.

ZIUSUDRA   I can understand that.

GILGAMESH   But the east was still barricaded against me by a serrated range of mountains arrayed in snow-laden thickets from end to end of the horizon, their myriad peaks as entangled with each other as with the clouds that never ceased to rake the highest sky. Only by turning south could I hope to get past around them. To make a clean escape I had to steal away without warning, apology, or pity. I made the best river boat I could secretly contrive and cut myself fifty punting poles to get through the marshes and off the shallows down to the open sea, by which I reasoned the whole continental barrier might be skirted. Then I could again travel as close as possible to Utu's daily path while keeping the pole star on my left by night. With a bolt of lady's cloth I hoped a breeze would ease my way. But the small winds were against me and the big winds tore it away with my mast.

—If I had another cloth I'd now know how to make it work to my advantage in any weather. Here at least I can cut a mast and spar.

MOTHER OF ALL   I'll not weave your shroud! I've lost too many sons to trust men's confidence.

GILGAMESH   Half of every day afloat I faced the blinding sun to fix my course. I ate and drank undigested fish from the fluid bellies of occasional sea birds, always defending myself from curious sharks

[Indicates his axe.]   with this handy invention of mine. At intervals on every island sojourn in my eastering—deflected by wind or current but always between the Crab and the Goat—I bartered knowledge or invention for my keep, but never again, no matter how long I tarried, did I forget my purpose. I do not forget it here, but I shall leave you the better for my visit.

ZIUSUDRA   Now wait a minute, Mister Noman!

[Suddenly rises and begins to pace about excitedly. Mother of All and Urshanabi stand up reflexively.]   This will be your last stop if you don't parley in good faith! You've been informed that I am wise! I will not be deceived! Double-bitted axe—tower—walls—canals—Uruk—Engidu! I am not ignorant of what the world hears! Are you a poet or an actor?

GILGAMESH   I cannot sing. But I sometimes take action.

ZIUSUDRA   You pretend to be Nimrod!

GILGAMESH   No, Engidu was Nimrod. I am Gilgamesh. I had hoped for the advantage of anonymity; but I have been too transparent in telling my story to a student of every science.

ZIUSUDRA   Then prove that you are Gilgamesh.

GILGAMESH   My seal, the Iso-recto-tetrahedron, a four-pointed jackstone.

ZIUSUDRA   I have heard of that amulet! But you may have stolen it from Gilgamesh.

GILGAMESH   Do you know the legend that I'm two-thirds god, only one third human?

ZIUSUDRA   Every human must have at least a trace of the gods that made his race.

GILGAMESH   My mother confessed that I was conceived under Utu's eclipse of Sine at a moment when her loves were equally divided. I had to choose between them for my god when I corrected Uruk's calendar.

ZIUSUDRA   Identity is never absolute, but the scope of your replies is sufficient. We shall have plenty of time to debate the heinous errors in your infamous measurement of years. —If you are Gilgamesh you can teach me how to write and read.

GILGAMESH   Then Urshanabi must help me build a boat, advise me of the local currents, and chart the eastern opening of this atoll.

MOTHER OF ALL   If Ziusudra agrees to that I'll weave your sail despite my warning. But I fear you're no less apt to kill yourself than any woman's reckless son.

URSHANABI   I'll show you how we fish the lagoon without an axe!

GILGAMESH   At half ebb tide the sand will be smooth
[To Ziusudra.]   and firm. Every day with a stick on the hard beach you will draw from your
[Points to the   head some of the pictures you hoard.
Isorectotetra-   With this stylus I will write their names
hedron on his   for you to compare before the tide
neck.]   returns to wash them out. All the words and pictures can then be inscribed on clay outside your head to work the thaumaturgy with at any time. Posterity will know forever the acts of resurrection by which you will have restored all living creatures to the earth.

ZIUSUDRA   Fame is not my motive. Is that the tal-
[Bends to   isman that's said to reconcile three with
examine it.]   four?

GILGAMESH   Also with the degrees of every azimuth. And with much else in reckoning. At your leisure I will decipher its many meanings.

ZIUSUDRA   If you were once a king, why now such a generous tutor?

GILGAMESH   I have no responsibility to keep religious secrets or vows of obedience like those that burden you. I have relieved myself of works. I've renounced my interest in power. I harbor no arcane jealousy. I exercise no wish either to know myself or to empty my mind of the pragmatical world. My mania is now confined to retrogression, leaving me in all else disinterested.

ZIUSUDRA   I pity your derangement. You are not the thoughtless brute of your reputation. But you cannot reach the meeting place of earth and sky without the vitalizing herb I shall give you to round out our interesting covenant. You must guard it for your life from diving albatross and breaching giant squid. They can sniff it at a hundred fathoms.

MOTHER OF ALL   Come, my dear. We must leave this brave guest for a while to gather incense for our meditation. We'll pray for him to acquire a taste for my palm wine that will at least prolong his holiday with us. —Urshanabi, let's celebrate with a new fish tonight. It goes without saying that there'll be yams, coconuts, and bananas for the other courses. Please sound the conch when everything's ready.

Mother of All leads Ziusudra off stage left.

URSHANABI   I must go fishing now. But tell me about this boat you have in mind.

GILGAMESH
[Picks up his axe by the head, handle downward.]

The tide looks about right: come on down and I'll draw a plan. —What's this herb the shaman has in mind for me?

URSHANABI
Gilgamesh &
Urshanabi go
off stage right.

Brier roses grow all along the shore. If you mind the thorns you can chop yourself a bushel of their hips.

BEROSUS
[Aside.]

In Babylon those thorny flowers are known as dog roses. Pyramus picked them for Thisbe.

TABLET TWELVE

Column One

[*Melchizedek*, tall, bearded, vested in white and gold, stands burning incense at a fieldstone altar outside his tent. *Berosus* sits with music instruments in his usual place.]

BEROSUS *Enter Gilgamesh,* stage right, *escorted by two of* *Melchizedek's* *armed scouts.*	This is Melchizedek, Amorite king of Canaan, priest of Elohim, come down from Shechem to the hills near Bethel.
MELCHIZEDEK	A prisoner from the west?
SCOUT I	A pirate called Noman, captured at sea off the coast of Kittim. Your ship's captain sends us to you with him.
MELCHIZEDEK	Well, another disappointment. I was hoping otherwise when I saw you coming. I'm awaiting the rich son of Shem who built this altar long ago. —You have no retainers or possessions at all?

219

GILGAMESH   A single free traveler, relieved of power but not a pirate.

SCOUT 2   He was carrying this axe.
[Hands over
Gilgamesh's
axe.]

GILGAMESH   It has saved my life on land and sea, but not as a weapon.

MELCHIZEDEK   You look as if you were once strong enough not to need one. But obviously you're not the shepherd warrior I've been looking for. You may keep your ambivalent axe. Let me see that jewel on your neck.

GILGAMESH   Just a piece of baked clay of no value to
[Exchanging   anyone but me.
the Isorecto-
tetrahedron for
the axe.]

MELCHIZEDEK   What image is this? No god that I have
[Examines the   seen before. It's an ugly naked figure.
IRTH intently
before distastefully handing it back.]

GILGAMESH   It's not to idolize but to bring to mind some thoughts.

MELCHIZEDEK   I'd like to hear those thoughts. We must converse at length before I let you go. Are you a wandering song-stitcher then, with a poor memory and no harp?

GILGAMESH   I'm sorry that I can't sing you my story. I was an autocrat, and will be again, but now I am alone. Almost twenty times with the polestar on my left I saw the

[Points in the direction from which he'd been brought.]

sun veer to the Crab and fall back to the Goat. Then after three oceans my course narrowed through two mountains into a narrow sea of stepping-stone islands—Trinacria, where they offered to worship my amulet; Caphtor, where they copied my axe; Kittim, where I taught them to draw plans; and others in between like even the Isle of Snakes where I found cordial haven in return for my advice. After all my previous solitary struggles, these heartening sojourns led me on a sea-path to these brine-ending forest-clad hills so sweetly watered by the clearest springs I have ever tasted. I hope that I have at last put angry waves behind me. What a discovery, this whole unbeknownst anti-world! The land of the rising sun! Already, in approaching, I have marveled at the outreach of its skills; now I have been brought to face the sovereign of its wisdom and power!

MELCHIZEDEK   What might you want of my goodwill?

GILGAMESH   Perhaps when I return from the further end of this land I may be allowed to fell some of these great trees to build a dragon ship for my voyage home. Down on the beach I would gather a crew of young sailors who'd like to see the old world and bear back to you more precious tokens of its glories than a humble axe. Meanwhile in gratitude for your generosity and friendship, as well as opening my mind to your ears I will open my mouth with navigational and military intelligence about how you can plant greater colonies along your landlocked western sea. —But how much further is the *eastermost?* Will I at last face Utu rising on the other side of those majestic heights, surely the last barrier to my goal?

[Points off stage left.]

MELCHIZEDEK   No one knows the end of that land across the valley. I can tell you only that there is a mountain pass to the steppes before you come to an endless river. Even now I am awaiting word of a great sheikh who comes with his tribe from somewhere down its banks. If you will wait with me for his account we may amplify each other's science.

GILGAMESH   At this stage of life I cannot linger. I must first find my half-father, the progenitor of time. The horizon has disappointed me so many times over these years that I am apt to be overtaken by weakness and irresolution before I can return to regain my strength. Until then I dare not sleep again, for fear of never waking.

MELCHIZEDEK   Your half-god Utu is but the Creator's creature! Speak of your other half.

GILGAMESH   My other half is human. My other third is lunar. Sine is my moon-father. I am not a worshiper of any other.

MELCHIZEDEK   Two at least approaches unity. It will not be entirely a sin to make you my guest for a day or two and hear all I can about a fabulous old world!

[To Scout 2.]   —Fetch the bread and wine.

Both
Scouts enter the tent and return with bread and wine, which they place before the altar.
[Melchizedek blesses the bread and wine at the altar and brings it to a low table center stage, at which they place two seats on either side. Gilgamesh sits facing east (stage right), opposite Melchizedek, each with a Scout nearby as servant. The axe is propped against the downstage center of the table, helve down, its head above the surface. As Gilgamesh and Melchizedek speak more confidentially the Scouts finish their own portions and discreetly bring another (unblessed) jar of wine to the table.]

—At my table you will eat and drink nothing better or worse than what is offered servants of the One God—he who has taken this fertile land from the perfidious Nephilim and given it to his righteous people.

—Humble bread from labor in the fields is holier than bloody meat, and I think you'll find the wine made from our grapes a more wholesome refreshment than the crude beer of idolaters. Let us celebrate the joining of two worlds under one God! Eat and drink in peace, stranger, and then ask for more. At least for a few hours shed your travail and favor me with the pleasure of your company.

GILGAMESH   A most welcome meal. Never have I tasted with such gusto!

MELCHIZEDEK   But, my friend, only an eagle can fly to the sun. No longer afloat with your gear, you won't be spared the stumbling blocks of gravity. You will be footsore and slow, girded with impediments, a pack on your back. And your axe can't feed you where game is rare and swift. You will need the distal weapon of a hunter. You shall have a longbow and its quiver of arrows if you are able to use them, won from a rock-slain giant. It is of no use here because none of our archers is strong enough to draw the string. Try it!
—Bring it out to him.

[Scouts fetch the bow and arrows from the tent, stay just long enough to watch in awe as Gilgamesh draws and shoots in a high arc eastward.]

GILGAMESH   I think I still have the strength to draw
Scouts   anyone's bow!
disappear.

MELCHIZEDEK   For your sustenance and safety on the eastern heaths—according to the will of God, if I'm not mistaken.

GILGAMESH   Then I thank you and Him for a timely gift. In my youth I was a bowman. And thanks to you for sharing the lordly purple-lipped invention of this draught! It warms my heart when I need rejuvenation. Vagrancy wearies the body more than manic battle does. I age with little aches and pains I never had before, none as definite or serious as sickness or wound. I used to hold a lion in my arms as easily as a cat; now even my legs don't recover all their strength when I'm fully rested in cloudless humor, charged with proleptic zest, and rejoicing in a spirit almost as clear and buoyant as when I had my dearest friend to double every muscle! I refrained from resisting your sailors only because I was loathe to test myself. Sometimes reason seems futile.

MELCHIZEDEK   Every mortal ages.

GILGAMESH   But I've survived the sea-world's fury only to face what I fear will be yet another continent of hazards! Is the orient endless? The sun is always rising or setting, constantly inviting, forever inaccessible! I feel no closer to the morning of the world than I did long ago in Dilmun. Has time no youth?

MELCHIZEDEK   Even youth grows old.

GILGAMESH   Even on a course against the sun's? Why shouldn't I be gaining time? Instead, fevers of thirst and starvation have left me weaker, though I stopped at every landing to recuperate and gather hips of roses. It's a sapping of lungs and sinew too subtle to notice in a month or year, enfeebling the very memory of full strength and wit—even of love and hope itself. Yet these swallows of your vine-juice call up pristine the idea of my end in view!

MELCHIZEDEK   Which I now perceive.

GILGAMESH   No, no, you mistake me! I have no wish for everlasting life. Better even to die without fame than live forever ruled by fate! It's more interesting before infirmity of mind to learn the mystery of time! The very thought of that success invigorates me! Too often now I sleep when I used to need no rest. —Ah that recalls the last dream I can remember: I spent many weeks on an island with the astrologer Ziusudra who had notions of the future. I had long since left him when he appeared at sea, standing in the stern to wake me from a sitting sleep within that dream. He warned me that even a god can die if he attacks another god (not to mention a demigod's mortality). He said: "Utu and Sine will eat up each other's light, one after the other. One must not watch his fathers fight!" Still dreaming, I was about to ask his meaning when suddenly with a downward surge both gunwales were seized by four raptorial limbs of a single loathsome intelligence I felt rising from beneath me as its other lurid arms groped like snakes for my basket of dogrose fruit. With my axe, left and right, I tried to free myself of the horror, terrified by underwater thrashing and bloody foam, but the boat of reeds was swamped, its length severed by my own blows. I saw Ziusu-dra's head calmly sinking as he continued to advise me. "Look, here comes a white whale to feed on the monster, and a dolphin to save you. Take your axe, but don't lose your life diving for the emptied basket."

I awoke on a shore I'd never seen before. Are you an interpreter of illusions? What did the old sage mean? What did the dream mean within which he meant it?

[Long silence as Melchizedek ponders. He suddenly rises in alarm.]

MELCHIZEDEK —Noman, tell me your real name!

GILGAMESH —Is that important?

[Taken aback, hesitates.]

MELCHIZEDEK If you expect my neutrality.

GILGAMESH Well then: I'm generally called Nimrod.

MELCHIZEDEK What made me dread to ask? A strange name I've heard before. What could have already carried it here?

GILGAMESH Perhaps it echoes some indistinct word you've dreamt.

MELCHIZEDEK No, there is only one cause of all things. It must have been an old warning among the words of God when I was distracted by immediate difficulties.

[Abruptly.] —Now the sun is down. I am disquieted by intimations of my indiscretion.

I must leave you now—for special pray alone, higher on the hill. In the morning we may not part as friends.

[To the Scouts.]
—Take your prisoner to the guest tent and see that he is provided for.

—Under my hospitality you need not fear to sleep. The bow is yours to keep. The Scouts will make you up a pack of food and water for sustenance on your way. But your quest is an impiety that I cannot countenance. A man might more easily try to watch one of God's oaks turning into the acorn that fathered it.

Melchizedek leaves. For a moment *Gilgamesh* stands still looking after him before he *is escorted off by the Scouts.*

Column Two

[*Gilgamesh* is prone on the ground, facing upstage center, drinking awkwardly from a river. His axe and bow are lying beside him. As he twists to cast the Iso-recto-tetrahedron off his neck he notices that a young *Shepherd* with a crook, spear, slingshot, and short sword (slung on a baldric) is watching him from stage left; but after a brief hesitation, driven by thirst, he bends again to drink with one arm behind him groping for the handle of his axe. *Berosus* is in his usual place with music instruments.]

BEROSUS   Gilgamesh is desperately drinking from a river. The bank is steep. He must take off the Iso-recto-tetrahedron lest he lose it in the water.

SHEPHERD 1
[Takes a cup from his belt, which Gilgamesh turns to accept. The Shepherd then gestures to someone behind him.]

Here, use this. If you drink too much all at once you'll get sick. Don't worry about the river running dry. You were lucky to get here before our flock muddied it all up. I won't let them come this far. Go ahead and take your fill.

—That's far enough. Water them down there by that double palm tree. Then we can pitch the tents up here. Send Peleg to tell the master.

[To Gilgamesh again.]

—I've been watching you come down from the desert. It looked as if you wouldn't make it this far. You must be a stranger to these parts. So are we, but we know enough to stay near the river, even when it turns north. Take your time. There are a thousand sheep, three hundred goats, a hundred asses, and all kinds of cattle to slow the camels down. They're still two or three miles behind. With all our men, women, children, and chattels, sometimes that takes a whole day. Thank God we don't keep swine!

[Gilgamesh finishes drinking with a sigh and hands back the cup.]

—Whatever possessed you to cross the desert? I suppose a desert's as deserted in the mountains as on the flats, and maybe harder going. I hope the Amorites aren't after you.

GILGAMESH   Thank you, my friend. I feel much better now. No one's chasing me. I've been heading east from the west the straightest way I can find. Down here it's hard to believe how cold I've been up among those rocks. I'm a stranger.

SHEPHERD 1   That's obvious. We're both strangers here.

GILGAMESH   Where are your people going with all those flocks and herds?

SHEPHERD 1   Going west from east, in a roundabout way. We must follow the fodder. The chief says we're going to settle in greener pastures somewhere over there. Did you see a land of milk and honey?

GILGAMESH   It's indeed a land of plenty.

SHEPHERD 1   More to the point: we lost a ewe, two lambs, and a kid last night. Did you see any wolves or lions on your way here?

GILGAMESH   Sorry, I haven't been looking for them these days—just hoppers or hoofers that I can eat. I haven't had a shot at one of those for the last five days. Nor even private property.

SHEPHERD 1   Oh I'm not accusing you! Here, have some figs. Not too many all at once!
[Gives figs. Gilgamesh eats voraciously as Shepherd watches him closely.]

GILGAMESH   Where are you people from? Did you live by yourselves with all that livestock at the end of the earth?

SHEPHERD 1
[Laughing.]   With more people than you can imagine! At least from what I've heard. I don't know much about it. I was born on the trek. My mother was one of the chief's favorites. All I know is that we usually give cities a wide berth, and even when we don't I have to stay outside with the sheep. I wouldn't know how to deal with a mess of people penned like cattle, even if they sacrificed to our God. I suppose they swarm and bleat like hind-legged goats and sheep! Not only the noise: I imagine cities stink to high heaven! But the chief and his wives don't seem to mind. He's just spent almost a month feasting and trading inside the biggest one yet. It's a relief to get moving again.

GILGAMESH
[Bowed in thought.]   Cities! When I came over the ridge today I saw something that looked like a city in the haze down there, but I thought it was a mirage. I've been having so many dreams and delusions that I was surprised to find there really was water quickening under the greenery I saw! —What's this river called?

SHEPHERD 1   The River. What else? The desert is the
desert. The river is the river. I think
cities have names, because there are
more than one. But that's no concern of
mine.

GILGAMESH   Where does the river go? Where's its
mouth?

SHEPHERD 1   Mouth! Where's its nose? Where's its
[Laughing   toes? You are an odd one, the way you
again.]   talk! Maybe the sun's too hot for you
here. You must be some kind of a poet.
What do you mean by "mouth"?

GILGAMESH   Where does it flow to? Where does the
water go?

SHEPHERD 1   How should I know? Where does the
land go? Where does the sun rise? You
do ask strange questions!

GILGAMESH   Do you know of another river?

SHEPHERD 1   Another river! There you go again! I
hope you don't read from the stars like
some daft minstrel singing to sunstruck
camel-drivers about another world in
the north or suchlike fantasies of the
fireside!

GILGAMESH   You did say there are several cities. So
they must have names to tell them
apart. What's that one called?

SHEPHERD 1   I never heard the name. Fishes don't have names. I don't know why cities need names. You can never be at more than one at a time. A city's just a big village, isn't it? All I've heard is that the king of this one is sometimes a woman.

GILGAMESH   Have you ever come across any holes of black water?

SHEPHERD 1   Oh, here and there. Even sheep are smart enough not to drink it. Where it's as thick as honey I've heard there are gentiles who even burn it! I once saw a gazelle get stuck in the devilish stuff. It took an hour to disappear. I wouldn't touch those stinking pits with a ten-foot pole, but last year I watched a city man smearing some of it on his boat with a stick. Maybe he was a wizard. Believe me, I didn't stick around to find out!

GILGAMESH   Well all people are not alike, since some live in cities. What are your folks called, or the people you work for?

SHEPHERD 1   They just call us Eber's tribe. I think he was my chief's great-great-great-grand-father somewhere down to the east or south of here. If I knew where that was I'd have answered your question about where the river goes to!

GILGAMESH
[Aside.]

What has disconnected the pieces of my mind? This bewilderment of old age frightens me! It's as if this boy is at the wrong end of things. Was my dear Eber a ghostly namesake five generations removed, across three oceans and a sea? But if New World names and migrations may repeat themselves by chance, is there another Lil-Amin to be found—or Engidu?

SHEPHERD I

You might ask the chief all your questions. He'll feed anyone who comes with knowledge of the west.

GILGAMESH

I thought I knew the world! What am I about to learn? —Some day, when I return to power, you will be rewarded. You may be opening my eyes to a wonder I cannot yet grasp.

SHEPHERD I

There are lots of things no one ever understands. Why does water move? They tell me what difference does it make, say your prayers, that's all you have to know. But of course I can see that you're no ordinary old fellow. My chief understands everything. He may give you a good dinner just to hear your story. I'll have Peleg take you to him when he's settled in his tent. I appreciate your gratitude but I don't count on your goodwill to better my lot. As for the refreshment, it's only the common courtesy we're all taught. You must have

[Gilgamesh betrays increasing agitation.]

already learned a lot from me by the process of elimination. For all I know, you may be a spy.

GILGAMESH

I begin to think I'm a spy from the world of dreams! But you and your help are real enough!

[Laughs, but no longer addressing the Shepherd, he throws himself again prone upon the river bank to see his reflection in the water, talking to himself. The Shepherd cocks his ear to listen.]

—Does the world repeat itself? Or is it merely accidental that the eastermost looks like the westermost, their rivers and landscapes so much alike? The end of the journey remains to prove that east is west and west is east! Yet I don't look any younger. The dog-rose saved my life at sea but does not erase the additions of time. It's not mere emaciation that unstrings my legs and shrinks my shoulders. It isn't the river's ripples that lays lines upon my face. Will I still be welcomed anywhere for the strengths of my prime? I've never relied on brawn as much as brain, but will that soon fail me too?

[To Shepherd.]

—It's impossible to get to the west by going to the east. Does the sun reverse and the pole star shift, and the zodiak too, to make me travel in a circle when I go straight toward a rim of the world that I can never reach? Do Utu and Sine deceive my senses in order to nullify this pursuit of reason? Or do I misinterpret my eyes with rash imagination? Maybe this terrestrial expanse and its weird transhumance goes on

forever, dismissing the question of sunrise anywhere. Has mankind always been deceived by reasoned facts?
—Does your leader retain a sagacious master of paradox? You think I'm old and crazy, but this is the first time in my life that I've been bereft of commonsense.

SHEPHERD 1 [Laughs.]   He is himself our savant. God speaks only to him. It's a poet you should ask for! You make it sound as if the world's a turning hornet's nest!

GILGAMESH   But if time's an arrow in the air, could one find himself about to be where he began—yet older? You who know the sky at dawn so well, what keeps the sunrise out of reach?

SHEPHERD 1   It's just too far away. Like the stars, which I've given up trying to count. Girls are more interesting.

GILGAMESH   Nevertheless I wish I could take you with me.

SHEPHERD 1 [Laughing.]   I'm willing. You've got me curious about why and what the river flows to. Ask the chief. But what could you trade him for me?

GILGAMESH   Knowledge of the Old World. He'd find it useful.

The younger
Shepherd 2, less well armed but carrying a flute, enters from stage left.

SHEPHERD I
[Laughing
again.]

He'd listen to the proposition if not forbidden by Elohim the One. He doesn't
seem to value my services very highly.
—Peleg, stand on that rock and watch
for you know what. I'm taking this gen-
tleman to the chief. If you see anything,
skirl on your pipe right loud. No need
for you to fight a lion! If I don't come
back to save your life, sooner or later
somebody else will be sent to relieve
your anxiety!

Peleg leaves
stage right.

—Did you have horses in the old
world? I don't much like herding camels
and dromedaries. They're haughty and
mean. But I'm sure I would be too if I
had them for my masters! Asses can be
difficult but at least you can feel sorry
for them. I should think horses would
be the best for an army.

GILGAMESH
[Aside.]

Norkid could make this clever fellow
his understudy! He's a bold cadet and
probably brave to boot. If my dreamy
way back to Uruk is not the path of a
mirage he'll be a good messenger and
companion—if I can teach him a spy's
discretion.

[To Shepherd.]

—You are confident enough. If we ever
stop long enough I'll teach you how to
make a bow from the finest wood and
bone. You'll soon be strong enough to
bend it. With string at ear, it will hum
like a purring paramour!

SHEPHERD I
[He tries
unsuccessfully
to draw
Gilgamesh's
bow, first with
one hand and
then with the
other.]

And I'm now old enough to have one! I
can already imagine ... all kinds of
love! ... If you show me how to handle
bow and axe, on both sides of my nose,
I'll teach you the javelin and sling, sinis-
ter or dexter!

GILGAMESH

[Points to his
pendant.]

I have no time left for superfluous skills,
but you have enough for them all. If
you're as bright as you sound, and not
too impatient, you'll do best for yourself
by mastering this stylus to scratch the
words of patrons and carry them to distant places for honorable reward. You
will have no competition.

SHEPHERD I

I've always had a secret yen for magic!
So on second thought, if you really
hope to be my new master without
promising so much as my keep, we
should stay out of the old sheik's way.
We'll avoid the hospitality of his righteous feast-bowl by skirting the camp
and coming back to the river further
downstream, out of sight behind his
back. I begin to doubt that he'd will-
ingly give me up for the bemusing
stories of a scarcely clothed vagabond!
We must show ourselves only in territory he's left forever. Then I can do
your bidding without hindrance. I'm
tired of sheep; they're all the same. I'd

like to learn new work and see strange gods. But I won't mind if friendly girls are all alike!

GILGAMESH I have weathered enough in plains as well as mountains. Let's hope you too will learn to cherish city walls for the advantages of civil enclosure! Every fleece in one fold—princess, priestess, and milkmaid!

[Aside, musing.] —According to one of my dreams I am about to transplant a green twig to an orchard in the past. I seem to have lost the idea of what I thought I sought— something that's made by all the changes of sky and earth and living creatures. Or was it what buoys all hope and doing? Am I losing more than I thought to gain? Is it living or unliving to trace an arrow against its motion?

SHEPHERD I Never mind my motives. —Hey, what wants to be filled when it's empty and wants to be emptied when it's full?

GILGAMESH Your belly.

SHEPHERD I I was thinking of girls, but that's a good guess! You are worthy to be my master— even without wages or food. But on to our first bivouac! What shall I call you?

GILGAMESH Noman is good enough for the present. What's your name?

SHEPHERD I   Ha! For the present I will answer to "Dumuzi". I'm an ambitious shepherd-boy risking longevity for adventure. What kind of dislodged beggar are you, whom I desert my tribe to serve? A fugitive for murder?

GILGAMESH   I'm a Sicani who has killed many men who were trying to kill me, and was made captain of fighting ships for the king of Caphtor, an island that rules half a middle sea. By war and bride-raids I won him fabled wealth, of which I was allowed a share. But I do not murder, and never before have I been a suppliant. I lost all my men and treasure, some to Phoenicians, some to the deep. This bow is the only gift I was able to save from my last whirlwind at sea. The Canaanites on shore drove me into the desert because they regard all seamen as Caphtors and all Caphtors as pirates.

SHEPHERD I   I know what islands are, in the river; but what exactly is a sea?

GILGAMESH   The sea is an eternally restless flood of irritable bitter water, green or gray or blue, that only fish can drink. It invests all continents and enlarges every breach with many-fingered hands. It heaves to the breath of Father Sine like an immense desert perpetually in motion. Though you sail for many moons in chaotic winds and currents you may never see a place. Except for Sine and Utu the gods themselves avoid it.

SHEPHERD I   I'm skeptical of whatever you may tell me, but, as you seem to think necessary, I'll accept your stories and definitions for the convenience in understanding each other. You've let slip that you know mountains; and you seem familiar with river-land: between us, I think you're a Kassite straggler trying to get back home through enemy lines much deeper than you'd expected!

GILGAMESH   What do you know about Kassites?

SHEPHERD I   Kassites are gentile freebooters who live by cruel rapine—fierce and cruel barbarians who toss babies on their swords and put villages to the torch. They are enemies of God! Nimrod was their khan.

GILGAMESH   Is that the lore of your tribe?

SHEPHERD I   That's what everybody says. I've always wondered how people hate what they don't learn for themselves. My mother told me the secret that her father was a Kassite prisoner. The people around here share most of that opinion, and they don't spare suspicious strangers by merely driving them into the desert. They'd assume you were a Kassite even if you weren't. We must disguise ourselves.

GILGAMESH   Maybe the reason you don't think like a shepherd is that you're half sheik by blood.

SHEPHERD I   But only one of many!

GILGAMESH   When we repossess my walls and tower I'll give you a job to your liking. Maybe my daughter's equerry. Meanwhile I intend to keep your attention with assignments and thoughts interesting enough to occupy whatever attention can be spared from your hereditary lust, which nevertheless I'll aid and abet with nostalgia.

SHEPHERD I   With all respect, to test that promise as we search for a safe spot to pitch our imaginary tent, I'll thank you for a fuller version of your outlandish story.

GILGAMESH   Then go keep your word to poor Peleg, and pack your kit. I'm sure you can find for us some useful artifacts too common in your camp to be missed, while I try to start a hare or something bigger. When we rejoin, and get a night of rest, I'll tell you how to teach yourself the ways of a city by going into the bazaars with your eyes and ears open until you find out who's wise among the foolish, and whom you can trust to answer a foreign trader's harmless questions. Then you can test yourself as a mummer. After a few days of taking in the local customs you'll know your way to the palace and where to hang around until you get access to the inside market.

SHEPHERD 1   Market for what, our camel-load of golden fleeces?

GILGAMESH   You are no longer a shepherd or wool merchant: you are apprentice to a Phoenician arms trader who wishes to sell one of the best battle-bows ever wrought by famous Caphtor craftsmen of well laminated wood and ivory, too stiff for ordinary men-at-arms to flex but destined for lords of the sea. It's worth an argosy, you may say in truth, and fit for some strong king who in his own chariot would lead the conquest of these riverine plains. Someone at the court will invite a display and demonstration of our uniquely precious treasure. Whatever the price they bargain for, it will buy a boat and all necessities for our escape down Euphrates—if that happens to be the gentile name of yonder river—to find what is where down there! Until you have elicited a royal summons this treasure will be the tool to provide us with flesh from field or stream.

[Aside.]   —He's no Engidu, but in this dream he stabs my heart like memories of young Lil-Amin! This clever Dumuzi serves well as an only son.

Gilgamesh & Shepherd 1 leave,
stage left.

Column Three

[Young princess *Enheduanna* sitting in her simple reception chamber. Elderly *Widow 1,* heavily veiled, and a couple of palace guards attend. *Berosus* stage right as usual.]

BEROSUS   This is Babylon when it was newly civilized, many centuries before I was born and educated there. It has not yet occurred to Sargon that he could overcome the southern cities on the river that were vaguely acknowledged to be the sources of all culture.

Shepherd 1 enters, carrying a rolled carpet on his shoulder, *followed by Gilgamesh.*

ENHEDUANNA   You are sure that no one knows what
[Shepherd 1 unrolls the carpet on the floor and reveals the bow, which is then handled as implied by the dialogue.]   you have inside that carpet? It must be a surprise for my father when he returns from driving off the Elamites. I hope it will be on his birthday! I'm always looking for such exotic presents as he'd never win in ordinary battle or get as tribute. On pain of death, it's a secret to be kept from his court and all the local merchants until after he's surprised by it—and before he can surprise me as usual with something in gold or lapis lazuli.

[She indicates Shepherd 1.]   —The king loves me all too well, but he knows I find grown-up men too coarse and hairy. He's never thought of bringing me a beautiful young slave like this one!

SHEPHERD I I'm a student, Madam, not a slave!

ENHEDUANNA You're not any older than I am! I'm glad you're free. Your legs look sturdy and hairless.

—Anyway, the surprise is as important as the bow itself. In a high king's life any novelty is rare, especially from a sheltered daughter! It has to be something I can meanwhile hide even from nosey chambermaids. Of course I trust my life and reputation with these three dears, but if your slimly curved machine is as manly as you claim, and I give you what you've asked for it, how can I be sure you'll refrain from boasting about my patronage until it's in my father's hands and you're a thousand miles away? Everyone knows that the Elamites and Kassites have spies out there in the plaza, and they'd love to spoil my fun!

GILGAMESH No one could see that he carried anything but a carpet. You can trust me as a cautious trader who has every reason to earn your continued protection, and to be at your future service from near or far. It is everywhere known that even rumor can't outdistance the effects of your displeasure.

ENHEDUANNA   Woe betide any betrayal of my conde-
scension! If word gets out too soon I'll
have every person now in this room
garroted and thrown to the river sharks
without a scruple of injustice. I mean it
too! I have more power than any of my
brothers because I'm the favorite, and
my father loves to see me exert his
authority. When I'm just a little older I
shall be the chief priestess of Inanna
and Sine for his empire. He promised
me!
—So you are the master of this lovely
boy? Where do you hail from? You're
better looking than other men your age.

GILGAMESH   I am Noman of Caphtor in the Middle
Sea where this bow was made for me
from the finest materials in the king's
arsenal. I had saved his country from
famine with shiploads of Sicani grain.
No other bow can shoot so far, if one's
strong enough to draw the string.

ENHEDUANNA   My father is the strongest man in the
world!

GILGAMESH   Then he will value it for more than the
surprise.

ENHEDUANNA   Try it, soldier.

[She gets up from her chair to handle the bow with feckless childlessness.

—You too.

—How can an old merchant be nearly as strong as my father!

Then the soldiers try without success to draw it. Gilgamesh finally shows them how easily he can do it.]

GILGAMESH   It's not strength but understanding. I have lived with this bow so long that I can feel its breathing. I know how to make it joyful.

ENHEDUANNA   Do you think I could make it laugh? I am a poet. With the words of my mouth I can make men laugh or cry.

GILGAMESH   Accept this royal weapon and on my return I shall bring you as a gift my tablet of runes with all the kennings that can be knotted among themselves a thousand ways to bring on smiles or tears, as you may choose to use them.

ENHEDUANNA
[Laughs and claps.]

What, do you trade in poetry too? Will your tablet tell me the story of Nimrod? I get nothing here but scraps or rumors about legends of what elders may have said when someone was too young to understand the words. The Eberews wouldn't tell me anything because of our religion!

—Do bards in the west sing of Nimrod?

GILGAMESH   In Canaan I think I heard that name used for a dragon to terrify children with.

ENHEDUANNA   Well I know he was a cruel tyrant! He betrayed his city to the Elamites and killed his own brother.

WIDOW 1   . . . his own brother. No! Giszax loved
[Wailing.]   him! . . . Elamites again!
    Call Norkid! . . . Father's soaking blood . . . cry my Kassite babies also dead! . . .
    Lil-Amin hates Gilgamesh gone from bed. . . . Enkidu lies in mother earth. . . .
    Mother Lil-Amin carries Semiramis to die a mother. . . . All mothers gone but one who flirts to be one. . . . No, no, no—not yet! . . . My eyes still hurt, hurt, hurt. . . .

ENHEDUANNA   Quiet, you crazy old fool! You tell me nothing! Such tantalizing gibberish, always the same! That's all I ever get out of her when she hears Nimrod mentioned—crooning repetitious unpoetic syllables! I hate her! Every now and then she falls into that agony of trance and torments me with her meaningless staccato screeches!

WIDOW 1   . . . screeches.

GILGAMESH   But every lamentation has its causes!

ENHEDUANNA   So of course I do love this half-crazed woman, alone of all those who wait on me in their own interest. They say she had served my grandmother, whose child she brought to the king my father. That child—whom she adored more than gods, to whom she devoted every breath her life—grew up to be my father's queen, young enough to be his daughter, and even in her youth ruled Babylon as his regent during endless foreign wars. Her I killed, my mother, by getting born too late. This shattered ancient, unable to tell her woe and no more useful to me than a mute as far as my mother is concerned, still loves me as much as she loved her—but sometimes when angry she makes me feel the guilt. Noman of the world, am I a murderer? Should I cast off my mother's savior and accord myself some peace of mind? Or should I keep her here in hope that some day her memory of the years before my birth will return? She must have been far braver and more loyal than I can even try to be. I cringe at the thought of looking at her bloody eye-sockets.

WIDOW I   . . . bloody eye-sockets.

ENHEDUANNA

[Bursting into
a peal of
laughter.]

Her memory is gone forever. —But why am I telling all this to a wandering merchant? . . . —Oh I know why! As a learned adventurer you can help me with the poem I mean to write about my mysterious origins. I'll reward you with jewels of your choice, or even private hugs and kisses, old as you are! —Now that would really give the palace something astonishing for their gossip!

WIDOW I

. . . their gossip.

GILGAMESH
[With signs of
impatience.]

Forgive me, but I can accept none of the gauds or kisses deserved by youth. You cannot give me time. I have heard enough to understand your wishes for intelligence of the past. For that purpose, and for mine, there's no need for me to linger here. If you provide us with a safe-conduct to your father's frontiers I will search the stuff of legend in every place along my way. Please let us take our leave without delay. If all goes well I'll stop here when I retrace my journey. Or at least Dumuzi here will carry you the story for your poem. Meanwhile you must study the art.

ENHEDUANNA
[Merrily
clapping her
hands.]

I'll make beautiful verses of what you find! Someday you'll hear how clever I am. My brothers don't even understand the stars, but I know how to interpret dreams! I can almost figure out the little marks that stand for acts and things on seals in my mother's jewel box. My father will depend on me for reading all kinds of signs! He wants me to learn for him, so I can keep accounts and make a lot of tablets to perpetuate his glory. What could be more interesting to future priests than stories? So find out for me all you can about that terrible Nimrod who hated the gods and made slaves of his own people. —If only women could be as free as men! I'd ride my barge all the way down the river to see for myself if there really is a tower almost touching heaven! But I can become famous right here by entertaining travelers who are not prevented from seeing elephants and giraffes, or mountains and sea-monsters, or shining walls!

WIDOW I   . . . shining walls.

ENHEDUANNA   But this boy is not dismissed quite yet. —I notice you did not try the bow, Dumuzi. Maybe you and I could do the trick together, before I let you go and keep the secret of my purchase—or tell the tale and make yourself the enemy of all my vengeful suitors. I'm still almost a virgin, but I know how to overcome your trembling in my presence. Such a body is nothing for a princess to disdain. You may learn something especially delightful and still get back to Noman before the gates close. —But you are free to spurn the simple curiosity of an imperial princess. I am not vindictive.

WIDOW 1   . . . not vindictive.

ENHEDUANNA   —In any case, Noman, here's payment
[Hands   for the bow, and something more in
Gilgamesh a   anticipation. In this city even my pri-
purse.]   vate affairs can't be kept secret for more than one turn of the sky. You have time to buy a boat, but you must cast off before dawn if you wish to stay afloat alive. Sometime soon this innocent messenger will take you safe-conduct tokens that can get a boat off and past the reach of jealous assassins.
—Well, do you choose to stay with me a while, my fresh darling?

WIDOW 1   . . . fresh darling.

Preceded by the guards, Enheduanna takes
up the bow and leaves, tenderly guiding
Widow 1 but glancing back over her
shoulder at *Shepherd 1,* who hesitates,
looking back and forth, *before following
her out.*

GILGAMESH

Gilgamesh circles
the stage in
agitation before
he *leaves.*

Does the tongue of that old woman
foretell? Or does it let loose fantastic
nightmares of the past? Do I seek past
or future? In the name of Utu, in the
name of Sine: who is, who was, or who
will be that New World Nimrod? —
Time's deception deepens. How can I
know which way the arrow flies?

TABLET THIRTEEN
[Badly damaged]

[An open space suggesting buried ruins on a truncated hill. *Widow 2* (as a ragged crone) kneels with a firedrill and a piece of socketed soapstone before an open fireplace and cooking pot, upstage left, near the inchoate statue of Engidu made by Gilgamesh in Tablet 10, now chipped and discolored beyond casual recognition. Engidu's bannerstone is set before it. Nearby stands the stone gnomon of a primitive sundial. *Berosus* in his usual position.]

BEROSUS   This high dune has been piled up and flattened by winds of sand swirling in contention. There is no evidence of the forlorn hamlet below it. The old woman formerly served as a priestess in the temple of Inanna (now known as Ishtar). She performs as a sacristine, preparing for a special liturgy of intercession as she addresses the effigy.

WIDOW 2
[As if
meditating
aloud.]

Nimrod, you were once our mighty hunter. If this day we are spared the bolts of heaven save us from slow starvation. We have served Inanna with the utmost means of our destitution. Humble offerings cannot measure our devotion. Listen to the frail voices of our faltering dance. Do not scorn the sacrificial tithes of our withered sustenance. Not a sheep or goat is left to offer. Instead the Optimates will bring seed cakes made with the sweepings of our barley. Dust is the only flour for bread we eat. The sun has sucked dry our well. A wineskin of river water is our libation.

Gilgamesh, nearly unrecognizable in desert dress, carrying his axe, *enters* from downstage right. [Until he speaks the Widow is unaware of his presence.]

—Let Inanna lay her hands upon your head as savior of her people. Plead that our sins have been thrust upon us. We always disavowed the sacrilege attributed to your name in error, but have too long suffered for. Only she can petition the Lord Enlil to absolve our submission to alien power and rescind impending doom.

—Pity the infirmity of our priest and the confusion of ancient Optimates; forgive the decline of women and the ignorance of men born too late to know how far we have fallen.

—I myself have barely strength enough to make this tinder hot. My husband used to say that I could inflame a rock.

GILGAMESH   Madam, do not be afraid. Can you tell me where I am? I am out of place in this naked landscape, and in time as well!

WIDOW 2   Well, you did startle me; it's been a long time since we've seen a stranger. But I can no longer fear any whispering man or daylight wraith. Speak up! I can still hear with one ear.

[Louder.]

GILGAMESH   Why do you live in arid desolation?

WIDOW 2   I stay on this sand hill to haunt it. You can't call it living, under the pitiless sky of a second widowhood, surviving much too long both daughters born to a soldier of fortune. They put a stop to happy memory.

GILGAMESH   Who, your own children?

WIDOW 2   The Elamites who raped them to death.

GILGAMESH   Why did they attack a godforsaken place like this? They are known to sack for riches.

WIDOW 2   For revenge. Once before they had seized this place but were driven out by others.

GILGAMESH   So, wreaking vengeance on your gods?

WIDOW 2   On us, for calling Kassites to displace them as our masters.

GILGAMESH   All for a knoll of sand half a mile from the river!

WIDOW 2   Euphrates was so angry about our canals and watergates that he changed his course.

GILGAMESH   I see no trace of irrigation works.

WIDOW 2   When fields are parched the floods level dikes and fill canals.

GILGAMESH   So famine was the bane?

WIDOW 2   The gods don't like artificial plenty. The farmers had to dig according to a dictator's plans. After he was gone our crops grew feeble, but it wasn't because they had failed to maintain the works. They discovered that the gods had sterilized their irrigated fields with salt.

GILGAMESH   Why do you stay up here without shade or shelter? Haven't you a village?

WIDOW 2   "Village" is a term too noble! Our hovels are down below. This windy summit
[Grunts a bitter laugh and points stage left.]
is the sunken crown of a citadel that once gathered clouds. Sandstorms spun this tumulus over rubble. You now stand where stood a nuptial bed lifted to the Lord God who has long since cursed us.

GILGAMESH   I grieve for every one of mankind's losses. Some day, if I can in this dream of mine, I'll help you recover—if I find my own city translated to the New World. But my memory of landscape is confused by too much travel. What do you call this place?

WIDOW 2   It's known as Warka to the caravans that now avoid it.

GILGAMESH   A name I never heard.

WIDOW 2   Naturally; since you're a stranger, like almost every other man on earth.

GILGAMESH   I thought I could get a better view by beaching my boat and climbing this hill, but the horizon doesn't seem any different from up here. Have you ever heard of Erech? If it's in this dream at all it must be further downstream than I estimated.

WIDOW 2
[Looking at him narrowly and hesitating.]

Oh, the nomads used to call this Erech! . . . The real name was Uruk, as women named it when the earth was young.

GILGAMESH
[Laughs.]

Your folks must have copied that lore. It's not surprising as a common kind of ekistic echo. Uruk is a famous city, emulated everywhere. A place to be celebrated with namesakes!

WIDOW 2
[Snorting. She labors with firedrill on soapstone socket.]

I doubt that, mister. A name reviled everywhere between the great two rivers! Disowned by our own Inanna and blighted by the highest god! We don't boast of names that label discord. You are a remarkably hapless traveler to find yourself here on the day of judgment. I am making ready for the liturgy

by kindling pure new fire, as my husband was taught in his religion. I'll
never be too inured by the fate of
women to tremble at what anyone's
gods still have in store.

GILGAMESH   What distinguishes today for fear?

WIDOW 2   Our priest's oracle has warned that the
moon will come like cancer to eat our
sun at noon today, in retribution for the
night this month when the sun stole
upon the moon to suppress our bright-
est light. When gods dispute each other
the catastrophe is always human.

GILGAMESH   Everywhere, even in ages of famine and
sorrow, both such prodigies have always
been idle threats, followed by neither
gain nor loss. But your priest is a very
good astrologer if he can predict of the
omens themselves. They at least can
have nothing to do with the sins of a
single spot in the wilderness!

WIDOW 2   I remember that kind of unbelief when
we were ruled by a godless khan. I tell
you, this is no ordinary pile of crumbled clay!

GILGAMESH   You are remembering other people's
dreams of another place. I know very
well how that can be. I too find myself
old. In fact I may be dreaming what
you say! But I hope I can provide for
you after I find my way back to the real

Uruk. Didn't I hear you say that river is Euphrates? —But I can't understand why it would be so hard to see a tileclad tower stepping halfway up to heaven even from as far away as Tigris is.

WIDOW 2
[Squinting up from her work.]

You now stand upon that landmark, old dreamer! On this dilapidated platform the priestess of Inanna was dedicated queen by the Lord of heaven. The blows of gods and follies of men have reduced it to the dust of clay that once elevated it to the bottom of heaven. From fields that once fed a wealth of trade you have climbed a skirt of wind-blown dirt!

GILGAMESH
[Peering in all directions.]

Can it be? And a whole city in this ruins too? You can't bewitch me, woman!

WIDOW 2

The walls were first to fail, undermined by floods no longer controlled to our advantage. Temple and palace crumbled. Then all our houses dissolved in mud. Our false prosperity left us desiccated ruins after the waters withdrew. When I was a little girl, before the khan and his northmen forced us to build those great monuments and gates, we were content with powerless rounds of toil and custom. By delivering us from enemies and raising us to glory he brought upon us grief and shambles!

GILGAMESH   This cannot be a lifetime's dream!

WIDOW 2   I was once a happy mother, but one affliction after another has humbled me to the state you see. Yet my widowhood and child-bereavement was no worse than the loss of our queen to the raiders who carried her off for a ransom that only Babylon might afford.

GILGAMESH   Had she no protection? Where were the Kassites then!

WIDOW 2
[Leaves her work to look more closely at his face, just as he takes sudden interest in the statue and banner-stone, walking across diagonally and dropping his axe to examine them on his knees. But with face averted he stops to listen closely.]
They were loyal palatines, but when we all began to believe that the tyrant who bound them to Uruk would never return they lost confidence in their waning power. He was no longer here to inspire general respect for foreign mercenaries. Off duty they were tormented by the people. Most of them were past their prime. By then their captain Norkid had become the queen's beloved consort, her source of secular power—her brave and just advisor, always guided by what he thought Gilgamesh would have wished; but his sword was no match for a hundred pitchforks in an alley of assassins while his few warriors were defending us at the walls. My husband was one of those devoted martyrs.

GILGAMESH   So Norkid's loyalty had as many edges as my axe! He occupied in full the place of his khan!

WIDOW 2

[Gets up to pace about the stage behind him with increasing interest.]

Why do you try to conceal your knowledge of our former times.

GILGAMESH

I remember you. Your man was Norkid's bravest.

—This numinous stone is Engidu! By the hand of Gilgamesh. Uncorrupted by worms or suppuration, free of posthumous filth! No carrion to mourn!

WIDOW 2

Enter Shepherd 1, downstage right from below, out of breath, standing still to listen unseen, armed with slingshot and javelin.

Engidu is a name forgotten. This is Nimrod the hunter, protector of my people, resurrected from his grave. — But I grieve no more for this dead Nimrod than for that vanished Nimrod who buried this one. It was he who led my husband to me and all my sorrows. So tell me no more! I want to guess nothing about you! But I warn you to go back to your boat before it's too late. You are imperilled by people who abominate all strangers, fixed in the hatred of fatal heresies implanted by foreigners who flouted their sacred law. The remaining citizens are old, but they are fierce, with too many stones and pitchforks even for a demigod. Save yourself from ignominious death. Then at least you may keep alive for humankind the memory of—whatever causes your quest.

GILGAMESH
[Looking up at
her.]

Is reason a false shadow of the world we really live in?

WIDOW 2

The people here may now have forgotten that I left the service of Inanna to marry a Kassite, but when there were no Troopers left they would have murdered my children if the Elamites hadn't speared them first. In folk memory the name Nimrod has come to mean either Gilgamesh or Engidu. But our implacable Rector isn't confused. He doesn't forget the details of humiliation under the regime that usurped his authority. What's left of my barren life, which I cherish only to remember its few truncated years of fruit, depends more upon his spark of charity for me than upon my sacerdotal craft. —Unlike our former king you appear to have no army to implement your offers of protection.

GILGAMESH

My latest army seems to have immolated himself to Inanna in Babylon.

WIDOW 2

I dare not speak well of Gilgamesh within local earshot, but I will say to you it was not his fault that my people refused to see the common good in which he left them. He broke the Tablets of Fate for the sake of liberating those who now remember nothing of him but their hatred. I am so used to the cumulating weight of terror and sorrow that I could not bear even an ounce of illusive hope, but if you should find that Gilgamesh is still alive somewhere in a world that I cannot imagine, tell him that at least two of Uruk's women, one high, the other low, did appreciate his reign.

GILGAMESH   You and the queen?

WIDOW 2   Lil-Amin and I. —Go to your boat, I say, before someone steals it! —I do not recognize you, but the priest's eyesight is not quite gone, and his enmity is enriched by four decades of vitriolic brooding. —So hurry down the way you came, stranger! He will soon be up here with the congregation. Even in this shrunken parish he can rile a plethora of fanatic men and ignorant sons to overpower an unprotected interloper, not to mention his gang of pious women with a bottomless supply of ceramic shards. If you haven't entirely lost your senses, sir, don't stand here and reminisce. Turn back while the day is still young. Get to your boat before someone steals it. —I can say no more! I cannot listen to you! I have no more wish to share the curse upon a man's head than I had to bring it down upon him!

GILGAMESH   I am very sorry that you've suffered so much for what seemed a heartless regime. —Perhaps it really was.

WIDOW 2 [Points upward.]	There's the first kite crossing the sun! Hurry, or you're lost indeed!
SHEPHERD 1 [Showing himself.]	No, an eagle! Good omen.
GILGAMESH	Dumuzi! You restore my faith in Eber's tribe! Has the princess of Babylon already had enough of your innocence?
SHEPHERD 1	No. Enheduanna sent me to learn the story for her poem. I was only a day behind your wake and spoor. This morning I found your empty boat and saw you in the distance clambering up this hill like a goat-hunter.
GILGAMESH	How long have you been standing there?
SHEPHERD 1	Long enough to hear what my mistress thought might be concealed by a mysterious trader. Apparently I'm as good at choosing a hero as I am at making love. Those are the two reasons she wants me back.
WIDOW 2 [She indicates stage right.]	Quiet, boy! I hear the procession coming up from the village! I won't give you away if you lie down and listen behind that pile of rubble. No matter what happens, don't look up at the sky! Per-

haps you at least will be spared as witness of our doom. The story will be all that's left of us, and should be told in Babylon.

GILGAMESH
[Shepherd 1 crouches in hiding. Gilgamesh passes him the IRTH to wear on his neck.]

Not the end of us, but another beginning! Engidu has been restored to me because I have breasted the arrow of time. In former life I broke up the council of gods and altered fate, but I have never despised them—only their submission to fate. I can face mutiny without your help. Yet if in my pursuit I've been mistaking death for time, you must save yourself to save my life as legend. Take my Iso-recto-tetrahedron as proof to Enheduanna that you were here to verify the transfiguration of Uruk!

BEROSUS
Rector enters stage left, solemnly but
nearsightedly, with *Optimates leading a number of men and women.* His clothes are shabby but he is still a powerful figure, wearing some shabby remains of ecclesiastical vestments. He carries the royal Rod and Ring.
[They do not notice Gilgamesh but form behind the Rector in a semicircle as he stands and genuflects to the Nimrod idol. Music by Berosus.]

The priest shows himself, rising head first from the hillside, followed by Optimates and people.

RECTOR

[He drops the Rod and Ring to take up the axe. Quickly peers about but sees neither the bannerstone nor Gilgamesh.]

Ahh! . . . A sinful omen to portend this hour's judgment of our fate? My eyes are half-burnt by study of the sun but I can see what I feel in my hand! What was Engidu's bannerstone is now the hateful axe that I know as well as my daily prayer even after forty years!

—Woman—defrocked Widow—is this the deed of a god? Or some nefarious trick of yours? I've never trusted the renewal of your vows!

WIDOW 2

Your Grace! The axe was here when I arrived this morning. I thought you had done magic during the night. I dared not touch that strange axe.

RECTOR

That axe is no stranger to me than Nimrod himself! I can smell his aura better than you can see the sky. There's been a change of air up here! Is this abomination a sign he's out of my reach in death? Or can it be that I'm to have my life's revenge before it ends?

[Turns to point immediately at Gilgamesh before the others follow his gaze.]

—Look around, all you fools! This axe wasn't dropped from heaven!

—There he is, usurper of my glebe! Defiler of the temple and enemy of the gods! Murderer of godgiven Engidu!

—But look, now he has no Traders or Troopers for schemers and bodyguards! No Eber to dispense invented law, no Norkid to execute decrees by force! Can't you see he's helpless? There are no longer any Eberews or Kassites to corrupt our language and defy the customs handed down by Inanna!

—Quick, some of you, fetch the hunting net! We may be spared at the last moment! Hurry! The unavenged gods themselves have led their enemy to us for immolation. In this last hour of doomsday we have in our hands the offering to expiate the pollution that has brought our city to the verge of extinction. —Here, this is work for a female priest. It's long since we've had flesh of any kind to sacrifice! The gods could not ask for better!

Several men hurry off, after some hesitation.

[He draws a knife and hands it to Widow 2. Gilgamesh is surrounded by the remaining people.]

WIDOW 2   But that is human blood! And if it's Gilgamesh's, said to be mingled with the blood of gods! The oldest laws forbid sacrifice of any victim that can plead in language!

RECTOR   Don't argue, woman! It's nearly noon-
              time! The Lord Enlil grants sacerdotal
              discretion to carry out his will. Demigod
              or antigod, Gilgamesh has attacked the
              gods we serve. But our atonement will
              fail if we don't work swiftly!

              —Strike once and collect his blood. I'll
              do the rest. Meanwhile stoke the fire to
              illuminate our Nimrod in the dark of
              the sun. Remember that this is the
              tyrant who violated our queen Lil-
              Amin, my lost sister. —At last he faces
              me without the powers of force!

GILGAMESH   Yes, my implacable adversary, I am

[Suddenly   alone, no longer tireless or confident in
steps forward my body's strength, but I do not plead.
and seizes the You are unfit for government, even in
Rod and   its service to your gods. Against your
Ring.]   will I built up Uruk, made it a ladder
              halfway up to heaven, taught it record-
              keeping and how to plan. I left the city
              famous for its prosperous peace. You
              have let it fall to ruin amidst fields of
              poisoned soil that once fed flocks and
              herds as well as populations through
              good years and bad. Always in the
              name of a religion made hateful you
              mouthed abhorrence of reason and har-
              bored   conspiracy   against   the
              sovereignty I earned by driving out
              those who had actually enslaved your
              people. For Lil-Amin's sake I was too

forgiving of your vengeful sedition, ignoring Eber's advice to scotch you at the roots.

—I did not set out to retrieve the Rod and Ring of a polity that's been poisoned by your pious hatred of changes made for the common good, but now that I find the beginning of my journey at its end I must do exactly that. I resume kingship over the ruins of my works wiser in the mystery of time. I have been at fault for pursuing my private thoughts and absenting myself from the constructive government of a discontented and selfish public that prefers the servitude of rote religion. I will begin again by sharing the wretched poverty to which you have reduced your congregation, but with less confidence in time the carrier of hope.

RECTOR
[Indicating the sundial.]

Time! There's no time now to hear more of your conceited folly! When that shadow passes zenith the Tablets of Fate you smashed in ostentation will be at last fulfilled! You will be dead before the sky grows dark.

GILGAMESH
[Addressing all the people.]

Without me, if heaven spares you the desert will not. There's only lingering death in your feeble efforts to survive. I'll make a softened calendar to strengthen and protect your—

RECTOR   No doubt with softened plans to pacify the gods! With the imposition of barbarous new tongues! With softened kilns of stinking naphtha from the devil's jakes to fire godsent clay! With softened rules and regulations, softened tolerance in specifications, and softened work-orders for the human machine! All under a haughty despot's softened lash!

GILGAMESH   Despot, perhaps—but no longer haughty, if I ever was.

RECTOR   You've trapped yourself on the apex of your orgulous architecture!

GILGAMESH   Time's circle ends where it begins—if this is really Uruk that I stand upon, if reason is disproved by fact, if the cosmos is irrational, or if logic's altered in duration! I now reset my mind. But I do not find the queen to whom I delegated power, only you her dissenting brother. That royal priestess was of more worth than all the power and glory of a shining tower, impregnable walls, elite archers, productive treasury, regulated canals, public granaries, and every art but those she made her own. You still claim leadership of the people and the sanction of heaven, so you I blame for the greatest loss of all.

RECTOR
[Incensed.]

You abandoned her! Your guards failed to protect her! I had no men-at-arms. Do not claim her love!

GILGAMESH

Men return with a gathered net. [With the help of others, directed by the Rector's gestures, they close in on Gilgamesh.]

I left this kingship to the queen, not to a narrowminded clergyman. I need claim nothing more. This woman, here, who served in her temple may remember that Lil-Amin and I were of one mind. Even Engidu could not share that!

RECTOR

Now I'd like to see your nostrils flare! The late Captain Norkid said the air around you used to glow in battle warp. Show us the red corona of your reputed fury!

WIDOW 2

[Gilgamesh exchanges the Rod and Ring for the knife.]

Here, take this knife! It's not for me to kill a hero. Cut the net and run!

OPTIMATES & PEOPLE

[Hostile of voice and gesture as they manage to throw the net over Gilgamesh.]

[The eclipse begins, gradually darkening the scene.

[Bewildered uproar. Cries of consternation and confusion at what may have seemed an unseen bolt from the sky.]

Shepherd 1 slings a bit of shard at a sector of the circle furthest from the Rector (who stands upstage right) and *kills Optimate 1,* thus diverting all attention from himself as he comes out of hiding to strike the Rector with his hurled javelin. Optimate 2 seizes the axe.]

RECTOR

Rector dies.

Kill Gilgamesh!

SHEPHERD I

Master, cut the net!

GILGAMESH
[Shouts, gasping, as he futilely attempts to cut his way out of the net. The Optimates and people surround him in a spiral dance as the men tighten the net around Gilgamesh and the women batter him with shards, bricks, or staves.]

Run, Dumuzi! . . . I'm all right! —My life began with thunder in mountains far away. . . . These are not my gods . . . the people do not love me . . . but I have made this my place! . . . —Go make yours in Babylon! —If you disobey me, my head and heart will feed the kites and suffer common worms in vain! My sempiternal public works have failed to last the lifetime of a man, but don't let my efforts vanish in the dust! . . . —I tell you, go! . . . Correct the memory of my love for Engidu! — Escape this mob . . .

—I don't claim fame for madcap feats . . . or for the love of Lil-Amin . . . but there will be space enough in time between my extinction and the world's . . . for arts not handed down from heaven! . . . —Don't let thoughts be lost to time. . . . You must be my voice until Enheduanna writes her poem. . . . Give the poet your words of mouth. . . . —If you perish, I fail . . . but if you live, so shall I. . . .

[Optimate 2 chops at Gilgamesh with the axe.] *Shepherd 1* hesitates until the eclipse is total; then, as Gilgamesh is hopelessly silenced, *runs off* downstage into the audience.

Gilgamesh dies. [Illumination slowly
returns. As Optimates gather around the
Rector's body the people, jeering, heap
dirt and shards upon Gilgamesh's body.]

WIDOW 2

[Plants the
Rod, Ring,
bannerstone,
and axe (head
upright) in or
upon the
burial mound.]

He did not die in exile. Some day they
will mourn their king. Unless our dance
is broken I am only the first to decorate
his tomb. Here the rainbow ends. Not
all things change: this hill will last forever.

BEROSUS

[As full light
returns.]

Three millennia have inherited an illiterate boy's witness. Let the world's
remaining centuries preserve this version of the legend.

JONATHAN BAYLISS was born in Arlington, Massachusetts, in 1926 and grew up during the Great Depression in Cambridge and rural Vermont. He studied at Harvard, served in the U.S. Navy during World War II, and finished his A.B. at the University of California at Berkeley.

While writing *The Tower of Gilgamesh* and *The Acts of Gilgamesh*, plays based loosely on the Sumerian epic, and GLOUCESTERMAN, his expansive fiction tetralogy, Bayliss earned a livelihood in positions involving sales analysis, accounting controls, systems, and management, beginning in 1950 at a Berkeley bookstore.

In the 1960s, as controller at Gorton's of Gloucester, the frozen-fish processor based in Gloucester, Massachusetts, he was a pioneer in developing integrated business applications for the IBM System 360. He also supervised the design and construction of Gorton's new headquarters building, working closely with the architect Eduardo Catalano. Bayliss left Gorton's in 1972, and with the financial assistance of a literary grant he devoted the following five years to full-time writing. Later he worked for the City of Gloucester as an executive aide to the mayor and as city treasurer, resuming full-time writing in 1985.

Bayliss was putting the finishing touches on his final novel when he died in Gloucester in 2009 at the age of 82.

The GLOUCESTERMAN series includes the novels *Prologos* (1999), *Gloucesterbook* (1992), *Gloucestertide* (1996), and *Gloucestermas* (2010), which may be read in any order. *The Tower of Gilgamesh* was originally published as part of *Gloucestertide* and *The Acts of Gilgamesh* as part of *Gloucestermas*.

Democratic Oak Tree, a collection of Bayliss's political essays and correspondence, was published posthumously by Drawbridge Press in 2016.

www.ingramcontent.com/pod-product-compliance
Lightning Source LLC
Chambersburg PA
CBHW050148120726
47903CB00002B/535